THE CATHEDRALS AND CHURCHES OF THE RHINE

LECTOR HOUSE PUBLIC DOMAIN WORKS

THE CATHEDRALS AND CHURCHES OF THE RHINE

FRANCIS MILTOUN
(MILBURG FRANCISCO MANSFIELD)

ISBN: 978-93-89701-77-7

Published: 1905

LECTOR HOUSE LLP
E-MAIL: lectorpublishing@gmail.com

COLOGNE CATHEDRAL

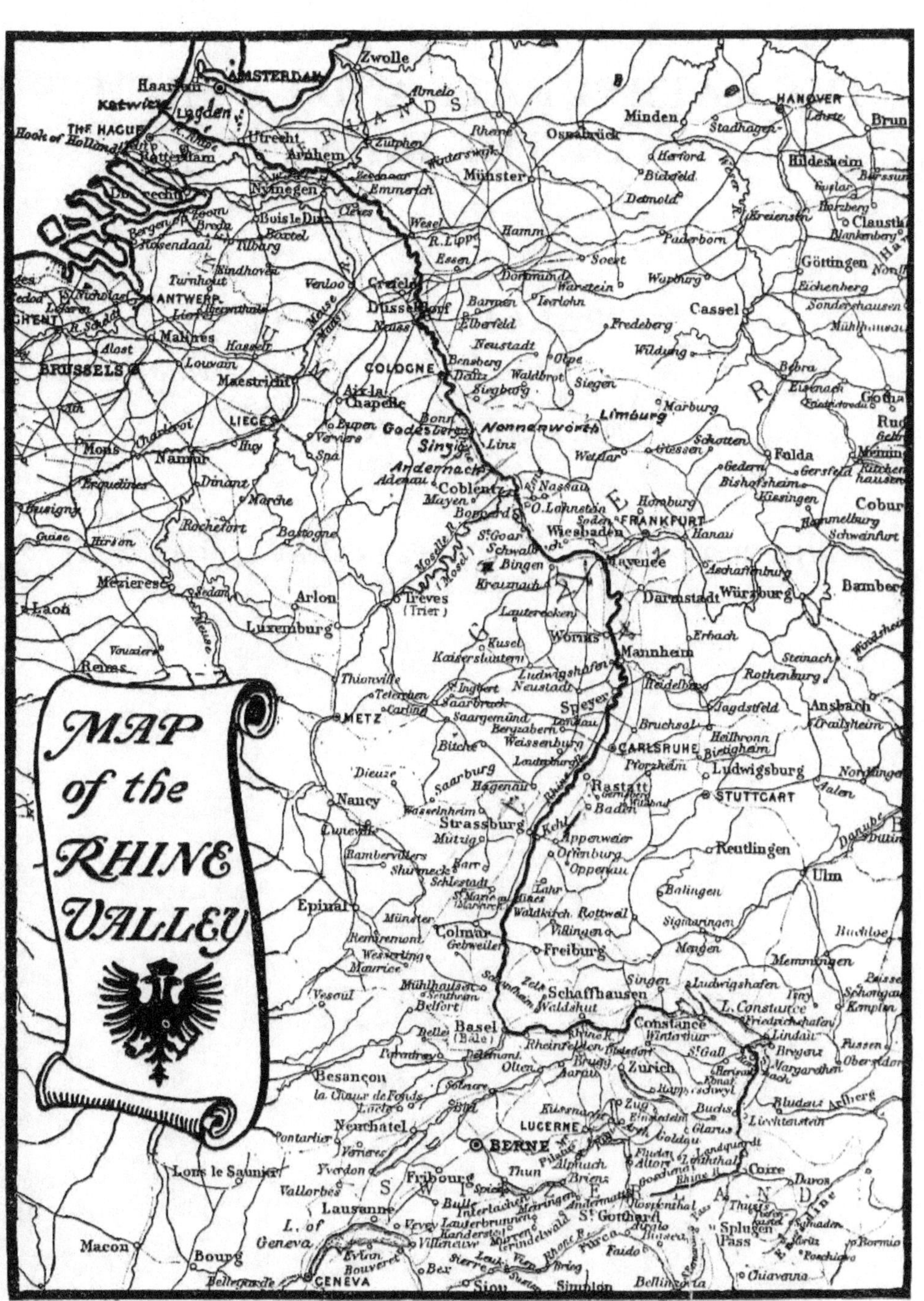

MAP OF THE RHINE VALLEY

THE CATHEDRALS AND CHURCHES OF THE RHINE

BY

FRANCIS MILTOUN

AUTHOR OF "THE CATHEDRALS OF NORTHERN FRANCE,"
"THE CATHEDRALS OF SOUTHERN FRANCE,"
"DICKENS' LONDON," ETC.

**WITH NINETY ILLUSTRATIONS, PLANS, AND DIAGRAMS, BY
BLANCHE MCMANUS**

1905

CONTENTS

LIST OF ILLUSTRATIONS

APOLOGIA

The Rhine provinces stand for all that is best and most characteristic of the ecclesiastical architecture of Germany, as contrasted with that very distinct species known as French pointed or Gothic.

For this reason the present volume of the series, which follows the Cathedrals of Northern and Southern France, deals with a class of ecclesiastical architecture entirely different from the light, flamboyant style which has made so many of the great cathedral churches of France preëminently famous.

Save Cologne, there is no great cathedral, either in Germany or the Low Countries, which in any way rivals the masterpieces of Paris, Reims, or Amiens, or even Lincoln or York in England.

Strasburg and Metz are in a way reminiscent of much that is French, but in the main the cathedrals and churches of the Rhine are of a species distinct and complete in itself.

Any consideration of the Rhine cities and towns, and the ecclesiastical monuments which they contain, must perforce deal largely with the picturesque and romantic elements of the river's legendary past.

Not all of these legends deal with mere romance, as the world well knows. The religious element has ever played a most important part in the greater number of the Rhine legends. For demonstration, one has only to recall the legends of "The Architect of Cologne," of "Bishop Hatto and His Mouse Tower on the Rhine," and of many others relating to the devout men and women who in times past lived their lives here.

In the Low Countries also,—at Liège, where we have "The Legend of the Liègeois," and at Antwerp, where we have "The Legend of the Blacksmith,"—and indeed throughout the whole Rhine watershed there is abundant material to draw from with respect to the religious legend alone.

As for the purely romantic legends, like "The Trumpeter of Sackingen" and "The Lorelei," there is manifestly neither room nor occasion for recounting them in a work such as this, and so, frankly, they are intentionally omitted.

In general, this book aims to be an account of the great churches in the Rhine valley, and of that species of architectural style which is known as Rhenish.

There is a fund of interesting detail to be gathered in out-of-the-way corners in regard to these grand edifices and their pious founders, but not all of it can be even catalogued here. The most that can be attempted is to point out certain obvious facts in connection with these ecclesiastical monuments, not neglecting the pictorial representation as well.

Tourists have well worn the roads along both banks of the Rhine, from Cologne to

Mayence, but above and below is a still larger and no less interesting country, which has been comparatively neglected.

Not all the interest of the Rhine lies in its castled crags or its vine-clad slopes, and not all the history of the middle ages emanated from feudal strongholds. The Church here, as in France, played its part and played it gloriously.

In this discussion of the Rhine churches from Constance to Leyden, the reader will be taken on what might, with considerable license, be called an "architectural tour" of the Rhine, and will be allowed to ramble along the banks of the river, looking in and out of the various religious edifices with which its cities and towns are crowded.

The valley of the Rhine is no undiscovered land, but it served the purpose of the author and the artist well, for it presents much variety of architectural form, and an abounding and appealing interest by reason of the shadows of the past still lingering over these monuments in stone.

THE CATHEDRALS AND CHURCHES OF THE RHINE

CHAPTER I

INTRODUCTORY

THERE is no topographical division of Europe which more readily defines itself and its limits than the Rhine valley from Schaffhausen to where the river empties into the North Sea.

The region has given birth to history and legend of a most fascinating character, and the manners and customs of the people who dwell along its banks are varied and picturesque.

Under these circumstances it was but to be expected that architectural development should have expressed itself in a decided and unmistakable fashion.

One usually makes the Rhine tour as an interlude while on the way to Switzerland or the Italian lakes, with little thought of its geographical and historical importance in connection with the development of modern Europe.

It was the onward march of civilization, furthered by the Romans, through this greatest of natural highways to the north, that gave the first political and historical significance to the country of the Rhine watershed. And from that day to this the Rhenish provinces and the Low Countries bordering upon the sea have occupied a prominent place in history.

There is a distinct and notable architecture, confined almost, one may say, to the borders of the Rhine, which the expert knows as Rhenish, if it can be defined at all; and which is distinct from that variety of pre-Gothic architecture known as Romanesque.

It has been developed mainly in the building of ecclesiastical edifices, and the churches and cathedrals of the Rhine valley, through Germany and the Netherlands, are a species which, if they have not the abounding popular interest of the great Gothic churches of France, are quite as lordly and imposing as any of their class elsewhere. The great cathedral at Cologne stands out among its Gothic compeers as the beau-ideal of our imagination, while the cathedral at Tournai, in Belgium—which, while not exactly of the Rhine, is contiguous to it—is the prototype of more than one of the lesser and primitive Gothic cathedrals of France, and has even lent its quadruple elevation to Notre Dame at Paris, and was possibly the precursor of the cathedral at Limburg-on-Lahn.

From this it will be inferred that the builders of the churches of the Rhine country were no mere tyros or experimenters, but rather that they were possessed of the best talents of the time.

There is much of interest awaiting the lover of churches who makes even the conventional Rhine tour, though mostly the tourist in these parts has heretofore reserved his sentiments and emotions for the admiration of its theatrical-looking crags and castles, the memory of its legends of the Lorelei, etc., a nodding acquaintance with the castle of Heidelberg, and a proper or improper appreciation of the waterside beer-gardens of Cologne. For the most part the real romance and history of the Rhine, as it flows from its source in the Grisons to the North Sea, has been neglected.

There are a large number of persons who are content to admire the popular attractions of convention; sometimes they evoke an interest somewhat out of the ordinary, but up to now apparently no one has gone to the Rhine with the sole object of visiting its magnificent gallery of ecclesiastical treasures.

No one glows with enthusiasm at the mention of these Rhenish churches as they do for the Gothic marvels of France. It is, of course, impossible, in spite of Cologne, Speyer, and Strasburg, that they should supplant Reims, Amiens, Chartres, or Rouen in the popular fancy, to say nothing of real excellence; for these four French examples represent nearly all that is best in mediæval church architecture.

The Reformation in Germany, with its attendant unrest, accounts for a certain latitude and variety in the types of church fitments, as well as—in many cases—an unconventional arrangement or disposition of the fabric itself.

One thing is most apparent with regard to German churches in general,—the fittings and paraphernalia, as distinct from the constructive or decorative elements of the fabric, are far more ornate and numerous than in churches of a similar rank elsewhere. It is true that the Revolution played its part of destruction along the Rhine, but in spite of this there is an abundance of sculpture and other ornament still left.

Thus one almost always finds elaborate choir-stalls, screens, pulpits, and altar-pieces, of a quantity and excellence that contrast strongly with the severe outlines of the fabric which shelters them.

In connection with the architectural forms of the ecclesiastical buildings of a country must invariably be considered such secular and civic establishments as represent the state in its relation to the Church, and along the Rhine, as elsewhere on the continent of Europe, the past forms an inseparable link which still binds the two. Here, not only the public architecture, but the private, domestic architecture takes on forms which, varied though they are, belong to no other regions. They are, moreover, only to be judged at their true value when considered as a thing of yesterday, rather than of to-day.

That portion of the Rhine which is best worth knowing, according to the ideas of the conventional tourist, is that which lies between Cologne and Mayence. This is the region of the travel-agencies, and of the droves of sightseers who annually sweep down upon the "legendary Rhine," as they have learned to call it, on foot, on bicycle, and by train, steamboat, and automobile.

Above and below these cities is a great world of architectural wealth which has not the benefit of even a nodding acquaintance with most new-century travellers.

To them Strasburg is mostly a myth, though even the vague memory of the part it played in the Franco-Prussian war ought to stamp it as something more than that, to say nothing of its awkwardly spired, but very beautiful and most ancient cathedral.

Still farther down the river one comes to Düsseldorf, that most modern of German cities. At Neuss, a short distance from Düsseldorf, is the church of St. Quirinus, which will live in the note-books of architectural students as one of the great buildings of the world.

It is a singularly ample river-bottom that is drained by the Rhine from its Alpine source to the sea, and one which offers practically an inexhaustible variety of charming environment; and here, as elsewhere, architecture plays no small part in reflecting the manners, customs, and temperaments of the people.

Of the value of the artistic pretensions of the people of Holland we have mostly obtained our opinions from the pictures of Teniers, or from the illustrated post-cards, which show clean-looking maidens bedecked in garments that look as though they had just been laundered. To these might be added advertisements of chocolate and other articles which show to some extent the quaint windmills and dwelling-houses of the towns. Apart from these there is little from which to judge of the wealth of architectural treasures of this most fascinating of countries, whose churches, if they are bare and gaunt in many ways, are at least as sympathetic in their appealing interest as many situated in a less austere climate. To realize this one has but to recall the ship-model-hung Kerk at Haarlem; the quaint little minaret which rises above the roof tops of Leyden; or, the grandest of all, the Groote Kerk of Rotterdam, which, on a cloud-riven autumn day, composes itself into varying moods and symphonies which would have made Whistler himself eager and envious of its beauty and grandeur.

In so far as this book deals only with the churches and cathedrals of the Rhine, and follows the course of the Neder Rijn and the Oud Rijn through Holland, there are but three Dutch cities which bring themselves naturally into line: Arnheim, Utrecht, and Leyden.

So far as Americans are concerned, there is a warm spot in their hearts for Old Holland, when they remember the brave little band of Pilgrims who gathered at Leyden and set sail from Delfthaven for their new home across the seas. This was but three hundred years ago, which, so far as the antiquity of European civilization goes, counts for but little. It is something, however, to realize that the mediæval architectural monuments of these places are the very ones which the Pilgrims themselves knew. It is true, however, that their outlook upon life was too austere to have allowed them to absorb any great amount of the artistic expression of the Dutch, but they must unquestionably have been impressed with the general appropriateness of the architecture around them.

GENERAL VIEW OF LEYDEN

Below Düsseldorf the topography and architectural features alike change rapidly, and the true Rhenish architecture of heavy arches, with an occasional sprinkling of fairy-like Gothic, really begins. Neuss, Essen, and all the Westphalian group of solidly built münsters speak volumes for German mediæval church architecture, while up the Rhine, past Düsseldorf, Cologne, Bonn, Königswater, Remagen, Sinzig, Andernach, Coblenz, and all the way to Mayence, and on past Schaffhausen to Basel are at least three score of interesting old churches as far different from those elsewhere as could possibly be imagined, and yet all so like, one to another, that they are of a species by themselves; all except the cathedral at Cologne, which follows the best practice of the French, except that its nave is absurdly short for its great breadth, and that its ponderous towers stand quite alone in their class.

In general, then, the cathedrals and churches of the Rhine form a wonderful collection of masterpieces of architectural art with which most well-informed folk in the world to-day should have a desire for acquaintanceship.

These often austere edifices, when seen near by, may not appeal to the popular fancy as do those of France and England, and they may not even have the power to so appeal; but, such as they are, they are quite as worthy of serious consideration and ardent admiration as any structures of their kind in existence, and they have, in addition, an environment which should make a journey among them, along the banks of the Rhine from its source to the sea, one of the most enjoyable experiences of life.

The Rhine loses none of its charms by intimate acquaintance; its history and legends stand out with even more prominence; and the quaint architectural forms of its cities are at least characteristically convincing.

Remains of every period may be found by the antiquary, from the time when the Roman eagle was triumphant throughout the dominion of the Franks to feudal and warlike times nearer our own day.

In addition, there are ever to be found evidences of the frugality and thrift of the Germans which preserve the best traditions of other days.

The love of the Rhineland in the breast of the Teuton is an indescribable sentiment; a confusion of the higher and lower emotions. It is characteristic of the national genius. We have been told, and rightly: "You cannot paint the Rhine, you cannot even describe it, for picture or poem would leave out half of the whole delicious confusion. The Rhine, however, can be set to music," and that apparently is just what has been done.

Everywhere one hears the music of the fatherland. Whether it is the songs and madrigals of the Church, or of the German bands in the Volksgarten, it is always the same, a light, irrepressible emotion which does much toward elucidating the complex German character.

Nowhere more than at Cologne is this contrast apparent. It is the most delightful of all Rhine cities. Usually tourists go there, or are sent there—which is about what it amounts to in most cases—in order to begin their "Rhine tour."

Before they start up-stream, they stroll about the city, pop in and out of its glorious cathedral, and perhaps one or another of its magnificent churches, — if they happen to be on their line of march to or from some widely separated points, — make the usual purchase of real *eau de Cologne*, — though doubtless they are deceived into buying a poor imitation, — and wind up in a river-side concert-garden, with much music and beer-drinking in the open.

This is all proper enough, but this book does not aim at recounting a round of these delights. It deals, if not with the Teutonic emotions themselves, at least with the expression of them in the magnificent and picturesquely disposed churches of both banks of the Rhine, from its source to the sea.

CHAPTER II

THE RHINE CITIES AND TOWNS

Cæsar, Charlemagne, and Napoleon all played their great parts in the history of the Rhine, and, in later days, historians, poets, and painters of all shades of ability and opinion have done their part to perpetuate its glories.

The Rhine valley formed a part of three divisions of the ancient Gaul conquered by the Romans: La Belgica, toward the coast of the North Sea; Germanica I., with Moguntiacum (Mayence) as its capital; and Germanica II., with Colonia Agrippina (Cologne) as its chief town. The Rhine was the great barrier between the Romans and the German tribes, and, in the time of Tiberius, eight legions guarded the frontier. The political and economic influences which overflowed from the Rhine valley have been most momentous.

The Rhine formed one of the great Roman highways to the north, and it is interesting to note that the first description of it is Cæsar's, though he himself had little familiarity with it. He wrote of the rapidity of its flow, and built, or caused to be built, a wooden bridge over it, between Coblenz and Andernach.

In the history of the Rhine we have a history of Europe. A boundary of the empire of Cæsar, it afterward gave passage to the barbarian hordes who overthrew imperial Rome. Charlemagne made it the outpost of his power, and later the Church gained strength in the cities on its banks, while monasteries and feudal strongholds rose up quickly one after another. Orders of chivalry were established at Mayence; and knights of the Teutonic order, of Rhodes, and of the Temple, appeared upon the scene. The minnesinger and the troubadour praised its wines, told of its contests, and celebrated its victories. The hills, the caves, the forests, the stream, and the solid rocks themselves were tenanted by superstition, by oreads, mermaids, gnomes, Black Huntsmen, and demons in all imaginable fantastic shapes.

Meantime the towns were growing under the influence of trade,—the grimy power that destroyed the feudal system. The Reformed religion found an advocate at Constance in John Huss even before Luther fulminated against Rome; printing was accomplished by Gutenberg at Mayence; and now steam and electricity have awakened a new era.

Cæsar, Attila, Clovis, Charlemagne, Frederick Barbarossa, Rudolph of Hapsburg, the Palatine Frederick the First, Gustavus Adolphus, and Napoleon have been victorious upon its banks. What more could fate do to give the stream an almost immortality of fame?

Little by little there were established on the banks of the river populous posts and centres of commerce. The military camps of Drusus had grown into settled communities, until to-day are found along the Rhine the great cities of Basel, Strasburg, Speyer, Worms, Mayence, Coblenz, Cologne, and Düsseldorf, and between them are dotted a series of cities and towns less important only in size, certainly not in the magnitude of their interest for the traveller or student, nor in their storied past.

Of the more romantic, though perhaps not more picturesque, elements of vine-clad slopes — where is produced the celebrated *Rheinwein* — the rapid flow of Rhine water, and the fabled dwelling-places of sprites and Rhinemaidens, there is quite enough for many an entertaining volume not yet written.

After traversing several of the cantons, the Rhine leaves Switzerland at Basel, on its course, through Germany and Holland, to the sea. Its chief tributaries are the Neckar, Murg, Kinzig, Aar, Main, Nahe, Lahn, Moselle, Erft, Ruhr, and Lippe. Its waters furnish capital salmon, which, curiously enough, when taken on their passage up the stream, are called lachse; but, when caught in autumn on their way down to the sea, are known as salmon. It affords also sturgeon, pike, carp, and lampreys. Its enormous rafts of timber have often been described, and should be seen to be appreciated. They often carried half a village of people, and were of great value. To-day these great rafts, however, are seldom seen.

In summer, when the tourist visits the river, its course is comparatively calm and orderly; it is only in spring, when the snows melt rapidly in Switzerland, that "Father Rhine" is to be beheld in all his might; for then the waters often rise a dozen feet above their common level. Its depth from Basel to Strasburg averages ten to twelve feet; at Mayence, twenty-four feet; at Düsseldorf, fifty feet.

To Basel, through the Lake of Constance from Grisons, the Rhine forms a boundary between Switzerland and the German States. From Basel to Mayence it winds its way through the ancient bed of the glaciers; and from Mayence to Bingen it flows through rocky walls to Bonn, where it enters the great alluvial plain through which it makes its way to the ocean.

The valley of the Rhine has been called the artery which gives life to all Prussia. The reason is obvious to any who have the slightest acquaintance with the region. The commerce of the Rhine is ceaseless; day and night, up and down stream, the procession of steamboats, canal-boats, floats, and barges is almost constant.

From the dawn of history both banks of the Lower Rhine had belonged to Germany, and they are still inhabited by Germans. Ten centuries or more have elapsed since the boundaries of the eastern and western kingdom of the Franks were fixed at Verdun, and, though the French frontier had frequently advanced toward Germany, and at certain points had actually reached the Rhine, no claim was advanced to that portion which was yet German until the cry of "To the Rhine" resounded through the French provinces in 1870-71.

Of course the obvious argument of the French was, and is, an apparently justifiable pretension to extend France to its natural frontier, but this is ill-founded on precedent, and monstrous as well. Against it we have in history that a *river-bed* is not a *natural* delimitation of territorial domination.

The Cisalpine Gauls extended their powers across the river Po, and the United States of America first claimed Oregon by virtue of the interpretation that a boundary at a river should give control of both banks, though how far beyond the other bank they might claim is unestablished.

Until the Lake of Constance is reached, with its fine city of the same name at its westerly end, there are no cities, towns, or villages in which one would expect to find ecclesiastical monuments of the first rank; indeed, one may say that there are none.

But the whole Rhine watershed, that great thoroughfare through which Christianizing and civilizing influences made their way northward from Italy, is replete with memorials of one sort or another of those significant events of history which were made doubly impressive and far-reaching by reason of their religious aspect.

The three tiny sources of the Rhine are born in the canton of Grisons, and are known as the Vorder-Rhein, the Mittel-Rhein, and the Hinter-Rhein.

At Disentis was one of the most ancient Benedictine monasteries of the German Alps. It was founded in 614, and stood high upon the hillside of Mount Vakaraka, at the confluence of two of the branches of the Rhine. Its abbots had great political influence and were princes of the Empire. They were the founders of the "Gray Brotherhood," and were the first magistrates of the region.

The abbey of Disentis was, in 1799, captured and set on fire by the French, but later on it was reëstablished, only to suffer again from fire in 1846, though it was again rebuilt in more modest style.

St. Trons was the former seat of the Parliament of Grisons. Its chief ecclesiastical monument is a memorial chapel dedicated to St. Anne.

On its porch one may read the following inscription:

> *"In libertatem vocati estis*
> *Ubi spiritus domini, ibi libertas*
> *In te speraverunt patres*
> *Speraverunt et liberasti oes."*

Coire was the ancient Curia Rhætiorum. It is the capital of the Canton of Grisons, and was the seat of a bishop as early as 562. The Emperor Constantine made the town his winter quarters in the fourth century.

The church of St. Martin, to-day belonging to the Reformed Church, is an unconvincing and in no way remarkable monument, but in what is known as the Episcopal Court, behind great walls, tower-flanked and with heavily barred gateways, one comes upon evidences of the ecclesiastical importance of the town in other days.

The walls of the ancient "ecclesiastical city" enclose a plat nearly triangular in form. On one side are the canons' residences and other domestic establishments, and on the other the cathedral and the bishop's palace.

In the episcopal palace are a number of fine portraits, which are more a record of manners and customs in dress than they are of churchly history.

The small cathedral and all the other edifices date from an eighth-century foundation, and are in the manifest Romanesque style of a very early period.

Within the cathedral are a number of funeral monuments of not much artistic worth and a series of paintings by Holbein and Dürer. As an art centre Coire would appear to rank higher than it does as a city of architectural treasures, for it was also the birthplace of Angelica Kauffmann, who was born here in 1741.

Ragatz is more famous as a "watering-place"—for the baths of Pfeffers are truly celebrated—than as a treasure-house of religious art, though in former days the abbey of Pfeffers was of great renown. Its foundation dates from 720, but the building as it exists to-day was only erected in 1665. The church, in part of marble, contains some good pictures. The abbey was formerly very wealthy, and its abbot bore the title of prince. The convent is to-day occupied by the Benedictines, to whom also the baths belong.

From this point on, as one draws near the Lake of Constance, the Alpine character of the topography somewhat changes.

The Lake of Constance was known to the Romans as *Brigantinus Lacus* or the *Lacus Rheni*. It has not so imposing a setting as many of the Swiss or Italian lakes, but its eighteen hundred square kilometres give the city of Constance itself an environment that most inland towns of Europe lack. The Lake of Constance, like all of the Alpine lakes, is subject at times to violent tempests. It is very plentifully supplied with fish, and is famous for its pike, trout, and, above all, its fresh herring.

From Basel the Rhine flows westward under the last heights of the Jura, and turns then to the north beneath the shelter of the Vosges, and, as it flows by Strasburg, first begins to take on that majesty which one usually associates with a great river.

At the confluence of the Main, after passing Speyer, Worms, and Mannheim, the Rhine first acquires that commercialism which has made it so important to the latter-day development of Prussia.

At the juncture of the Main and Rhine is Mayence, one of the strongest military positions in Europe to-day. Here the Rhine hurls itself against the slopes of the Taunus and turns abruptly again to the west, aggrandizing itself at the same time, to a width of from five hundred to seven hundred metres.

Shortly after it has passed the last foot-hills of the Taunus, it enters that narrow gorge which, for a matter of 150 kilometres, has catalogued its name and fame so brilliantly among the stock sights of the globe-trotter.

No consideration of the economic part played by the Rhine should overlook the two international canals which connect that river with France through the Rhône and the Marne.

The first enters the Rhine at Strasburg, a small feeder running to Basel, and the latter, starting at Vitry-le-François, joins the Marne with the Rhine at the same place, Strasburg.

GENERAL VIEW OF DÜSSELDORF

On the frontier of the former *département* of the Haut-Rhin, one may view an immense horizon from the south to the north. From one particular spot, where the heights of the Vosges begin to level, it is said that one may see the towers of Strasburg, of Speyer, of Worms, and of Heidelberg. If so, it is a wonderful panorama, and it must have been on a similar site that the Château of Trifels (three rocks) was situated, in which Richard Cœur de Lion was imprisoned when delivered up to Henry VI. by Leopold of Austria.

To distract himself he sang the songs taught him by his troubadour, to the accompaniment of the harp, says both history and legend, until one day the faithful Blondel, who was pursuing his way up and down the length of Europe in search of his royal master, appeared before his window.

Some faithful knights, entirely devoted to their prince, had followed in the wake of the troubadour, and were able to rescue Richard by the aid of a young girl, Mathilde by name, who had recognized the songs sung by Blondel as being the same as those of the royal prisoner in the tower of the château. When the troubadour was led to the door of the prince's cell, he heard a voice call to him: "*Est-ce toi, mon cher Blondel?*" "*Oui, c'est moi, mon seigneur,*" replied the singer. "*Comptez sur mon zèle et sur celui de quelques amis fidèles—nous vous deliverons.*"

The next day the escape was made through an overpowering of the guard; and Richard, in the midst of his faithful chevaliers, ultimately arrived in England.

Blondel had meanwhile led the willing Mathilde to the altar, and received a rich recompense from the king.

As the Rhine enters the plain at Cologne, it comes into its fourth and last phase.

Flowing past Düsseldorf and Wesel, it quits German soil just beyond Emmerich, and enters the Low Countries in two branches. The Waal continues its course toward the west by Nymegen, and through its vast estuary, by Dordrecht, to the sea.

The Rhine proper takes a more northerly course, and, as the Neder Rijn, passes Arnheim and Utrecht, and thence, taking the name of Oud Rijn, fills the canals of Leyden and goes onward to the German Ocean.

Twelve kilometres from Leyden is Katwyck aan Zee, where, between colossal dikes, the Rhine at last finds its way to the open sea. More humble yet at its tomb than in the cradle of its birth, it enters the tempestuous waters of the German Ocean through an uncompromising and unbeautiful sluice built by the government of Louis Bonaparte.

For more than eleven hundred kilometres it flows between banks redolent of history and legend to so great an extent that it is but natural that the art and architecture of its environment should have been some unique type which, lending its influence to the border countries, left its impress throughout an area which can hardly be restricted by the river's banks themselves.

We know how, in Germany, it gave birth to a variety of ecclesiastical architecture which is recognized by the world as a distinct Rhenish type. In Holland the architectural forms partook of a much more simple or primitive character; but they, too, are distinctly Rhenish; at least, they have not the refulgence of the full-blown Gothic of France.

Taine, in his "Art in the Netherlands," goes into the character of the land, and the struggle demanded of the people to reclaim it from the sea, and the energy, the vigilance required to secure it from its onslaughts so that they, for themselves and their families, might possess a safe and quiet hearthstone. He draws a picture of the homes thus safeguarded, and of how this sense of immunity fostered finally a life of material comfort and enjoyment.

All this had an effect upon local architectural types, and the great part played by the valley of the Rhine in the development of manners and customs is not excelled by any other topographical feature in Europe, if it is even equalled.

Coupled to the wonders of art are the wonders of nature, and the Rhine is bountifully blessed with the latter as well.

The conventional Rhine tour of our forefathers is taken, even to-day, by countless thousands to whom its beauties, its legends, and its history appeal. But whether one goes to study churches, for a mere holiday, or as a pleasant way of crossing Europe, he will be struck by the astonishing similarity of tone in the whole colour-scheme of the Rhine.

The key-note is the same whether he follows it up from its juncture with salt water at Katwyck or through the gateway of the "lazy Scheldt," via Antwerp, or through Aix-la-Chapelle and Cologne.

Sooner or later the true Rhineland is reached, and the pilgrim, on his way, whether his shrines be religious ones or worldly, will drink his fill of sensations which are as new and different from those which will be met with in France, Italy, and Spain as it is possible to conceive.

From the days of Charlemagne, and even before, down through the fervent period of the Crusades, to the romantic middle ages, the Rhine rings its true note in the gamut, and rings it loudly. It has played a great part in history, and to its geographical and political importance is added the always potent charm of natural beauty.

The church-builder and his followers, too, were important factors in it all, for one of the glories of all modern European nations will ever be their churches and the memories of their churchmen of the past.

CHAPTER III
THE CHURCH IN GERMANY

There have been those who have claimed that the two great blessings bestowed upon the world by Germany are the invention of printing by Gutenberg, which emanated from Mayence in 1436, and the Reformation started by Luther at Wittenberg in 1517. The statement may be open to criticism, but it is hazarded nevertheless. As to how really religious the Germans have always been, one has but to recall Schiller's "Song of the Bell." Certainly a people who lay such stress upon opening the common every-day life with prayer must always have been devoted to religion.

The question of the religious tenets of Germany is studiously avoided in this book, as far as making comparisons between the Catholic and Protestant religions is concerned.

At the finish of the "Thirty Years' War," North Germany had become almost entirely Protestant, and many of the former bishops' churches had become by force of circumstances colder and less attractive than formerly, even though many of the Lutheran churches to-day keep up some semblance of high ceremony and altar decorations. It is curious, however, that many of these churches are quite closed to the public on any day but Sunday or some of the great holidays.

In the Rhine provinces the Catholic faith has most strongly endured. In the German Catholic cathedrals the morning service from half-past nine to ten is usually a service of much impressiveness, and at Cologne, beloved of all stranger tourists, nones, vespers, and compline are sung daily with much devotion.

The ecclesiastical foundation in Germany is properly attributable to monkish influences. Between the Rhine and the Baltic there were no cities before the time of Charlemagne, although the settlements established there by the Church for the conversion of the natives were the origin of the communities from which sprang the great cities of later years.

The monkish orders were ever a powerful body of church-builders, and north of the Alps in the eleventh and twelfth centuries, even though they were the guardians of literature as well as of the arts, the monks were possessed of an energy which took its most active form in church-building.

Whatever may have been the origin of the later Romanesque church-building, whether it was indigenous to Lombard Italy or not, it was much the same in Spain, France, England, and Germany, though it took its most hardy form in Germany, perhaps with the cathedral of Speyer (1165-90), which is one of the latest Romanesque structures, contemporary with the early Gothic of France. In Italy, and elsewhere along the Mediterranean, the pure Romanesque was somewhat diluted by the Byzantine influence; but northward, along the course of the Rhine, the Romanesque influence had come to its own in a purer form than it had in Italy itself.

Here it may be well to mention one pertinent fact of German history, in an attempt to show how, at one time at least, Church and state in Germany were more firmly bound together than at present.

The Germanic Empire, founded by Charlemagne in the year 800, was dissolved under Francis II., who, in 1806, exchanged the title of Emperor of Germany for that of Emperor of Austria, confining himself to his hereditary dominions.

In the olden times the Germanic Empire was in reality a league of barons, counts, and dukes, who, through seven of their number, elected the emperor.

These electors were the Archbishops of Mayence (who was also Primate and Archchancellor of the Empire), Trèves, and Cologne; the Palatine of the Rhine, Arch-Steward of the Empire; the Margrave of Brandenburg, Arch-Chamberlain; the Duke of Saxony, Arch-Marshal; and the King of Bohemia, Arch-Cupbearer.

In no part of the Christian world did the clergy possess greater endowments of power and wealth than did those of the Rhine valley.

The Archbishop of Cologne was the Archchancellor of the Empire, the second in rank of the electoral princes, and ruler of an immense territory extending from Cologne to Aix-la-Chapelle; while the Archbishops of Mayence and Trèves played the rôle of patriarchs, and were frequently more powerful even than the Popes.

All the bishops, indeed, were invested with rights both spiritual and temporal, those of the churchman and those of the grand seigneur, which they exercised to the utmost throughout their dioceses.

St. Boniface was sent on his mission to Germany in 715, having credentials and instructions from Pope Gregory II. He was accompanied by a large following of monks versed in the art of building, and of lay brethren who were also architects. This we learn from the letters of Pope Gregory and the "Life of St. Boniface," so the fact is established that church-building in Germany, if not actually begun by St. Boniface, was at least healthily and enthusiastically stimulated by him.

Among the bishoprics founded by Boniface were those of Cologne, Worms, and Speyer, and it may be remarked that all of these cities have ample evidences of the round-arched style which came prior to the Gothic, which followed later. If anything at all is proved with regard to the distinct type known as Rhenish architecture, it is that the Lombard builders preceded by a long time the Gothic builders.

Charlemagne's first efforts after subduing the heathen Saxons was to encourage their conversion to Christianity. For this purpose he created many bishoprics, one being at Paderborn, in 795, a favourite place of residence with the emperor.

Great dignity was enjoyed by the Bishop of Paderborn, certain rights of his extending so far as the Councils of Utrecht, Liège, and Münster. The abbess of the monastery at Essen, near Düsseldorf, was under his rule; and the Counts of Oldenberg and the Dukes of Clèves owed to him a certain allegiance; while certain rights were granted him by the cities of Cologne, Verdun, Aix-la-Chapelle, and others.

These dignities endured, in part, until the aftermath of the French Revolution, which was the real cause of the disrupture of many Charlemagnian traditions.

After the Peace of Lunéville, in 1801, the electorates of Cologne, Trèves, and Mayence were suppressed, together with the principalities of Münster, Hildesheim, Paderborn, and Osnabrück, while such abbeys and monasteries as had come through the Reformation were dissolved.

Besides Charlemagne's bishoprics, others founded by Otho the Great were suppressed.

Upon the restoration of the Rhenish provinces to Germany in 1814, the Catholic hierarchy was reëstablished and a rearrangement of dioceses took place. A treaty with the Prussian state gave Cologne again an archbishopric, with suffragans at Trèves, Münster, and Paderborn, and Count Charles Spiegel zum Desenburg was made archbishop. Other provinces aspired to similar concessions, and certain of the suppressed sees were reërected.

The Lutherized districts, north and eastward of the Rhine, were very extensive, but the influence which went forth again from Cologne served to counteract this to a great extent.

The Catholic hierarchy in Germany is made up as follows:

ARCHBISHOPRICS	SUFFRAGANS
Posen and Gnesen	Kulm and Ermeland
Breslau	
Olmütz	
Prague	
Cologne	Hildesheim, Osnabrück, Münster, Paderborn, Fulda, Limburg, Trèves, Mayence.
Freiburg in Breisgau	Würtemberg, Augsburg,
Munich and Freising	Passau and Ratisbon.
Bamberg	Würzburg, Eichstadt, and Speyer, and the Vicariat of Dresden.
Strasburg and Metz	

The religious population of Germany to-day is divided approximately thus: Protestants, 63 per cent; Catholics, 36 per cent; Jews, 1 per cent.

The reign of the pure Gothic spirit in church-building, as far as it ever advanced in Germany, was at an end with the wars of the Hussites and the Reformation of Luther. During these religious and political convulsions, the Gothic spirit may be said to have died, so far as the undertaking of any new or great work goes.

Just as we find in Germany a different speech and a different manner of living from that of either Rome or Gaul, we find also in Germany, or rather in the Rhenish provinces, a marked difference in ecclesiastical art from either of the types which were developing contemporaneously in the neighbouring countries.

The Rhine proved itself a veritable borderland, which neither kept to the strict classicism of the Romanesque manner of building, nor yet adopted, without question, the newly arisen Gothic of the twelfth and thirteenth centuries.

Architecture and sculpture in its earliest and most approved ecclesiastical forms undoubtedly made its way from Italy to France, Spain, Germany, and England, along the natural travel routes over which came the Roman invaders, conquerors, or civilizers—or whatever we please to think them.

Under each and every environment it developed, as it were, a new style, the flat roofs and low arches giving way for the most part to more lofty and steeper-angled gables and openings. This may have been caused by climatic influences, or it may not; at any rate, church-building—and other building as well—changed as it went northward, and sharp gables and steep sloping lines became not only frequent, but almost universal.

The Comacine Masters, who were the great church-builders of the early days in Italy, went north in the seventh century, still pursuing their mission; to England with St. Augustine, to Germany with Boniface, and Charlemagne himself, as we know, brought them to Aix-la-Chapelle for the work at his church there.

The distinctly Rhenish variety of Romanesque ecclesiastical architecture came to its greatest development under the Suabian or Hohenstaufen line of emperors, reaching its zenith during the reign of the great Frederick Barbarossa (1152-90).

The churches at Neuss, Bonn, Sinzig, and Coblenz all underwent a necessary reconstruction in the early thirteenth century because of ravages during the terrific warfare of the rival claimants to the throne of Barbarossa.

Frederick, one claimant, was under the guardianship of Pope Innocent III., and Philip, his brother, was as devotedly cared for by the rival Pope, Gregory VIII. Finally Innocent compromised the matter by securing the election of Otho IV., of Brunswick.

With that "hotbed of heresies," Holland, this book has little to do, dealing only with three centres of religious movement there.

Holland was the storm-centre for a great struggle for religious and political freedom, and for this very reason there grew up here no great Gothic fabrics of a rank to rival those of France, England, and Germany. Still, there was a distinct and most picturesque element which entered into the church-building of Holland in the middle ages, as one notes in the remarkable church of Deventer. In the main, however, if we except the Groote Kerk at Rotterdam, St. Janskerk at Gouda, the archbishop's church at Utrecht, and the splendid edifice at Dordrecht, there is nothing in Holland architecturally great.

CHAPTER IV

SOME CHARACTERISTICS OF
RHENISH ARCHITECTURE

IT cannot be claimed that the church-building of one nation was any more thorough or any more devoted than that of any other. All the great church-building powers of the middle ages were, it is to be presumed, possessed of the single idea of glorifying God by the building of houses in his name.

"To the rising generation," said the editor of the *Architectural Magazine* in 1838, "and to it alone do we look forward for the real improvement in architecture as an art of design and taste."

"The poetry of architecture" was an early and famous theme of Ruskin's, and doubtless he was sincere when he wrote the papers that are included under that general title; but the time was not then ripe for an architectural revolution, and the people could not, or would not, revert to the Gothic or even the pure Renaissance—if there ever was such a thing. We had, as a result, what is sometimes known as early Victorian, and the plush and horsehair effects of contemporary times.

In general, the churches of Germany, or at least of the Rhine provinces, are of a species as distinct from the pure Gothic, Romanesque, or Renaissance as they well can be. Except for the fact that of recent years the *art nouveau* has invaded Germany, there is little mediocrity of plan or execution in the ecclesiastical architecture of that country, although of late years all classes of architectural forms have taken on, in most lands, the most uncouth shapes,—church edifices in particular,—they becoming, indeed, anything but churchly.

The Renaissance, which spread from Italy just after the period when the Gothic had flowered its last, came to the north through Germany rather than through France, and so it was but natural that the Romanesque manner of building, which had come long before, had a much firmer footing, and for a much longer period, in Germany, than it had in France. Gothic came, in rudimentary forms at any rate, as early here as it did to France or England; but, with true German tenacity of purpose, her builders clung to the round-arched style of openings long after the employment of it had ceased to be the fashion elsewhere.

This, then, is the first distinctive feature of the ecclesiastical edifices erected in Germany in the twelfth and thirteenth centuries when the new Gothic forms were elsewhere budding into their utmost beauty.

One strong constructive note ever rings out, and that is that, while the Gothic was ringing its purest sound in France and even in England, at least three forces were playing their gamut in Germany, producing a species quite by itself which was certainly not Gothic any more than it was Moorish, and not Romanesque any more than was the Angevin variety of round-arched forms, which is so much admired in France.

One notably pure Gothic example, although of the earliest Gothic, is found in Notre Dame at Trèves, with perhaps another in the abbey of Altenburg near Cologne; but these are the chief ones that in any way resemble the consistent French pointed architecture which we best know as Gothic.

The Rhenish variety of Romanesque lived here on the Rhine to a far later period, notably at Bonn and Coblenz, than it did in either France or England.

German church architecture, in general, is full of local mannerisms, but the one most consistently marked is the tacit avoidance of the true ogival style, until we come to the great cathedral at Cologne, which, in truth, so far as its finished form goes, is quite a modern affair.

In journeying through Northeastern France, or through Holland or Belgium, one comes gradually upon this distinct feature of the Rhenish type of church in a manner which shows a spread of its influence.

All the Low Country churches are more or less German in their motive; so, too, are many of those of Belgium, particularly the cathedral at Tournai and the two fine churches at Liège (Ste. Croix and the cathedral), which are frankly Teutonic; while at Maastricht in Holland is almost a replica of a Rhenish-Romanesque basilica.

At Aix-la-Chapelle is the famous "Round Church" of Charlemagne, which is something neither French nor German. It has received some later century additions, but the "octagon" is still there, and it stands almost alone north of Italy, where its predecessor is found at Ravenna, the Templars' Church in London being of quite a different order.

Long years ago this Ravenna prototype, or perhaps it was this eighth-century church of Charlemagne's, gave rise to numerous circular and octagonal edifices erected throughout Germany; but all have now disappeared with the exception, it is claimed, of one at Ottmarsheim, a fragment at Essen, and the rebuilt St. Gérêon's at Cologne.

These round churches—St. Gérêon's at Cologne, the Mathias Kapelle at Kobern, and, above all, Charlemagne's Münster at Aix-la-Chapelle, and others elsewhere, notably in Italy—are doubtless a survival of a pagan influence; certainly the style of building was a favourite with the Romans, and was common even among the Greeks, where the little circular pagan temples were always a most fascinating part of the general ensemble.

It would hardly be appropriate in a book such as this to attempt to trace the origin of Gothic, as we have come to know that twelfth and thirteenth century variety of pointed architecture, which, if anything, is French pointed. It has been plausibly claimed that, after its introduction into France and England, it developed into the full-blown style of the fourteenth century, which so soon fell before the Renaissance in the century following.

In Germany the process, with differences with regard to its chronology, was much the same.

It has been the fashion among writers of all weights of opinion to break into an apparently irresistible enthusiasm with regard to Gothic architecture in general, and this, so far as it goes, is excusable. Most of us will agree that "the folk of the middle ages had fallen in love with church-building, and loved that their goldsmith's work, and ivories, their seals, and even the pierced patterns of their shoes should be like little buildings, little tabernacles, little 'Paul's windows.' Some of their tombs and shrines must have been conceived as little fairy buildings; and doubtless they would have liked little angels to hop about them all alive and blow fairy trumpets."

In the building of the great cathedrals it must certainly be allowed that there is an element that we do not understand. Those who fashioned them worked wonder into them; they had the ability which children have to call up enchantment. "In these high vaults, and glistening windows, and peering figures, there was magic even to their makers."

Gothic art must ever, in a certain degree, be a mystery to us, because we cannot entirely put ourselves in the place of the men of those times. "We cannot by taking thought be Egyptian or Japanese, nor can we again be Romanesque or Gothic," nor indeed can we explain entirely the *motif* of Burmese architecture, which, appearing as a blend of Chinese and Indian, stands out as the exotic of the Eastern, as does the Gothic of the Western, world.

Only in these latter two species of architectural art does stone-carving stand out with that supreme excellence which does not admit of rivalry, though one be pagan and the other Christian.

Germany, above all other nations of the middle ages in Europe, excelled in the craftsmanship which fashioned warm, live emotions out of cold gray stone, and to-day such examples of this as the overpowering and splendid cathedrals at Cologne, Ratisbon, Strasburg, and Münster rank among the greatest and most famous in all the world, in spite of the fact that their constructive elements were reminiscent of other lands.

The distinction between French and German building cannot better be described than by quoting the following, the first by James Russell Lowell on Notre Dame de Chartres, and the second by Longfellow on the cathedral at Strasburg:

CHARTRES

"Graceful, grotesque, with every new surprise of hazardous
caprices sure to please, heavy as nightmare, airy, light as fun,
imagination's very self in stone."

STRASBURG

". . . A great master of his craft,

> Ervin von Steinbach; but not he alone,
> For many generations laboured with him,
> Children that came to see these saints in stone,
> As day by day out of the blocks they rose,
> Grew old and died, and still the work went on,
> And on and on and is not yet completed."

The first is typical of the ingenuity and genius of the French, the second of the painstaking labour of the Teuton; what more were needed to define the two?

"In Germany and throughout all the territory under the spell of Germanic influence the growth of Gothic was not so readily accomplished as in France," says Gonse.

"At best such Gothic as is to be seen at Bacharach, Bonn, Worms, etc., is but a variety, so far as the vaulting goes, of superimposed details on a more or less truthful Romanesque framework. At Mayence, Roermond, and Sinzig, too, it is the domical vault which still qualifies the other Gothic essentials, and so depreciates the value of the Gothic of the Rhine valley when compared with that of the Royal Domain of France."

The range of mediæval art and architecture has been said to run between the fourth century and the fourteenth, or from the peace of the Church to the coming of the Renaissance.

This is perhaps definite enough, but the scope is too wide to limit any special form of art expression, so that one may judge it comparatively with that which had gone before or was to come after.

Mostly, mediæval art groups itself around the two distinct styles of Byzantine and Gothic, and they are best divided, one from the other, by the two centuries lying between the tenth and the twelfth.

In truth, the architecture of Germany, up to the end of the tenth century, was as much Byzantine as it was Romanesque, and the princes and prelates alike drew the inspiration for their works from imported Italians and Greeks, a procedure which gave the unusual blend that developed the distinct Rhenish architecture.

The Popes themselves gave a very material aid when they sent or allowed colonies of southern craftsmen to undertake the work on these great religious edifices of the Rhine valley.

The grander plan of the cathedrals at Speyer, Worms, Mayence, Basel, and even Trèves are all due somewhat to this influence, and for that reason they retain even to-day evidences of these foreign and even Eastern methods, though for the most part it is in the crypt and subterranean foundations only that this is found.

Carlovingian architecture was perhaps more indigenous to Germany than to any other part of the vast Empire. "This extraordinary man," as the historians speak of Charlemagne, did much toward developing the arts.

In the southeast, the Grecian Empire was already become decrepit in its influences, and a new building spirit was bound to have sprung up elsewhere. "If

Charlemagne," says Gibbon, "had fixed the seat of his empire in Italy, his genius would have aspired to restore, rather than violate the works of the Cæsars." He confined his predilections to the virgin forests of Germany, however, and he despoiled Lombardy to enrich his northern possessions; as witness the columns which he brought from Ravenna and Rome wherewith to decorate his palace and church at Aix-la-Chapelle.

No country has preserved finer or more numerous examples of Romanesque architecture than Germany. The Rhine was so powerfully under Roman sway that it adopted as a matter of course and without question quite all of the tenets and principles of the Romanesque; not only with respect to ecclesiastical structures, but as regards civil and military works as well.

On the Rhine, as in Lorraine, Lyonnaise, and Central France, the Romanesque endured with little deviation from Latin traditions till quite the end of the thirteenth century.

Later, in the Gothic period, Germany returned the compliment and sent Zamodia of Freiburg and Ulric of Ulm to lend their aid in the construction of the grand fabric at Milan; and John and Simon of Cologne to Spain to erect that astonishingly bizarre cathedral at Burgos.

Beginning with the revival of the arts in Italy, the Renaissance German architects, in other countries than Germany, were apparently few in number and not of their former rank.

Not alone did Italy aid Germany in the erection of ecclesiastical monuments, but France as well, with the Norman variation of the Romanesque and the later developed Gothic, sent many monkish craftsmen to lend their aid and skill. Their work, however, was rather the putting on of finishing touches than of planning the general outlines.

German architecture on the Rhine then was but a development and variation of alien importations, which came in time, to be sure, to be recognized as a special type, but which in reality resembled the Lombardic and the Romanesque in its round-arched forms, and the Gothic of France in its ogival details. German architecture in time, though not so much with respect to churches, even went so far as to imitate the rococo and bizarre ornamentation fathered and named by the Louis of France.

Germany was a stranger to the complete development of Gothic architecture long after it had reached its maturity elsewhere; so, too, it was quite well into the fifteenth century before the slightest change was made toward the interpolation of Renaissance details, and even then it was Renaissance art, more than it was Renaissance architecture, which was making itself felt.

The Renaissance came to Germany through the natural gateway of the north of Italy; although it spread perhaps to some extent from France into the Rhine district.

In truth, German Renaissance has ever been heavy and ugly, though undeniably imposing. In both the ecclesiastical and the secular varieties it lacked the lightness and grace which in France, so far as domestic architecture went, soon developed into a thing of surprising beauty.

What the Renaissance really accomplished in Germany toward developing a new or national style is in grave doubt, beyond having left a legacy of bizarre groupings and grotesque and superabundant ornament. In France the case was different, and, while in ecclesiastical edifices the result was poor and banal enough, there grew up the great and glorious style of the French Renaissance, which, for civic and private buildings of magnitude, has never been excelled by the modern architecture of any land.

In Germany proper, as well as in Switzerland, one finds house-fronts and walls covered with paintings, which is certainly one phase of Renaissance art. But the brush alone could not popularize the new style, and in religious edifices, at least, the Renaissance, as contrasted with the earlier Romanesque, never attained that popularity along the Rhine that it did in France or England, or even in Belgium.

Civic architecture took on the new style with a certain freedom, but religious architecture almost not at all. Possibly the "Thirty Years' War" (1618-48) had somewhat to do with stunting its growth; certainly no church-building was undertaken in those years, and they were the very ones in which, elsewhere, the Renaissance was making its greatest headway.

Another very apparent reason is that, as the major part of the population became Protestant, the need of a beautiful church edifice itself, as a stimulus to the faith, had grown less and less. There was a steady growth, perhaps one may as well say a great development, in civil architecture throughout Germany at this time, but, to all intents and purposes, from the early seventeenth century onward, the founding and erecting of great churches was at an end.

If one would study the Renaissance in Germany he must observe the town halls of such cities as Cologne, Paderborn, or Nuremberg, or the great châteaux or castles, such as are best represented by ruined Heidelberg.

Of religious architecture Renaissance examples are practically lacking; the most convincing details along the Rhine being seen in the western tower of the cathedral at Mayence.

At Hildesheim, at Nuremberg, and at Prague there are something more than mere "evidences" of the style, and throughout Germany, as elsewhere, there are many sixteenth and seventeenth century accessories, such as altars, *baldaquins*, tombs, and even entire chapels, which are nothing but Renaissance in motive and execution. But there are no great Renaissance ground-plans, façades, or *clochers*, which are in any way representative of the style which crept in to ring the death-knell of Gothic in France and England.

Perhaps it is for this reason alone that the great Gothic cathedral at Cologne was completed at a late day with no base Renaissance interpolation in its fabric.

CHAPTER V

THE ACCESSORIES OF GERMAN CHURCHES

Up to the tenth century the German basilicas were but copies of the Roman variety. Even the great cathedral at Trèves, with its ground-plan a great square of forty metres in extent, was but a gross imitation of the Romanesque form of the sixth century.

Later, in the eighth century, came the modified Byzantine form which one sees at Aix-la-Chapelle.

With the eleventh century appeared the double-apsed basilicas, but, from this time on, German ecclesiastical art divorced itself from Latin traditions, and from the simple parallelogram-like basilica developed the choir and transepts which were to remain for ever.

The crypt is a distinct and prominent feature of many German churches. On the Rhine curious and most interesting examples are very frequent, those at Bonn, Essen, München-Gladbach, Speyer, Cologne (St. Gérêon's), Boppart, and Neuss being the chief. All of these are so constructed that the level of the pavement is broken between the nave and choir, producing a singularly impressive interior effect.

Speyer has the longest, and perhaps the largest, crypt in all Germany.

Where the edifice has remained an adherent of Catholicism, the crypt often performs the function of a place of worship independent of the main church, it being fitted up with one or more altars and frequently other accessories.

As the crypt, instead of being only an occasional attribute, became general, squared, or even more rude, capitals replaced the antique and classical forms which Christian Italy herself had adopted from pagan Greece.

These squared or cubic capitals are particularly noticeable at Neuss, at München-Gladbach, in St. James at Cologne, and in the old abbey of Laach.

Towers came to be added to the west fronts, but the naves often remained roofed with visible woodwork, though, by the end of the century, the stone-vaulted nave had appeared in the Rhine district, and the pillars of pagan birth had given way to the columns and *colonnettes* of Latin growth.

What is known as the German manner of church-building had more than one distinguishing feature, though none more prominent than that of the columns of the nave and aisles. The naves were in general twice the width of their aisles, and the bays of the nave were made twice the width of those of the aisles. Hence it followed that every pier or column carried a shaft to the groin of the aisle vault, and every alternate one a shaft to the nave vault; and so grew the most distinct of all German features of Romanesque church-building, alternate light and heavy piers in the nave.

It is on the Rhine, too, that one comes upon occasional examples of rococo architectural decoration, a species which sounds as though it might originally have been Italian, but which was originally French. At its best it is seldom seen on the exterior, but on inside walls and porticoes, notably at Bruchsal on the Rhine, one sees a frankly theatrical arrangement of ornate details.

By the twelfth century the particular variety of Romanesque architecture which had developed, and still endures, in the Rhine valley had arrived at its maturity.

The thirteenth century saw the interpolation and admixture of Gothic, which elsewhere, in France in particular, was making such great strides.

Towers multiplied and became lighter and more graceful, and great Gothic arched windows gave place to round-headed ones, though scarcely ever to the entire exclusion of the latter variety.

The species of cross-bred style which forms the link between the Romanesque and Gothic abounds along the Rhine, and examples are frequently encountered.

The semicircular apsides, with a decorative band beneath the cornices of the exterior galleries, are also a distinctly Rhenish detail. They are to be seen in St. Peter's at Bacharach, at St. Castor's at Coblenz, St. Martin's at Cologne, the cathedral at Bonn, in St. Quirinus at Neuss, and again at Limburg.

The Rhenish bell-towers are a variety distinct from the towers and spires usually met with, and often terminate suddenly, as if they were unfinished.

Finally, there are a number of churches in this region which offer the singular, though not unique, disposition of a chevet showing a triple apsis. Notable examples of this style are St. Maria in Capitola, St. Andrew and St. Martin at Cologne, and St. Quirinus at Neuss.

The churches of the Rhine valley are abundantly supplied with steeples, often in groups far in excess of symmetry or sense, as for instance the *outré* group at Mayence, which is really quite indescribable.

The Apostles' Church at Cologne, the cathedrals at Mayence, Speyer, and Worms, and the abbey church of Laach all have wonderfully broken sky-lines; while those with great central towers, such as at Neuss, or the parish church of Sinzig, form another class; and the slim-spired churches at Andernach and Coblenz yet another. St. Martin's at Cologne is another single-spired church, but it rises from its three apses in quite a different manner from that of St. Quirinus at Neuss, and must be considered in a class by itself.

The minster at Bonn, though having three steeples, is not overspired, like that of Mayence,—indeed, it is perhaps one of the most picturesque, if somewhat theatrical, of all the spired churches of the Rhine, excepting always Limburg. The open-work spire of Freiburg is unequalled in grace by even that of Strasburg, whatever may be the actual value of its constructive details.

WORMS CATHEDRAL

A marked type of German church architecture is that species of building known as the *Hallenkirche*. The variety is found elsewhere, even in France, but still it is distinctively German in its inception.

Usually they are of the triple-naved variety, *i. e.*, a nave with its flanking aisles, with the aisles nearly always of the same height as the principal nave.

There are two great churches of this order—though lacking aisles—in France, the cathedrals at Rodez and Albi in the south.

Mostly these great halled churches exist in Westphalia, where there is a fine example in the cathedral at Paderborn, and again there is St. Ludger at Münster, and many others. In one form or another the type is frequently met with through-out Germany, and is therefore to be considered as a distinct German architectural expression.

In summing up, then, one may well conclude that German church architec-ture, in its general plan and outline, is not of the amazing beauty of the French, and is in a way lacking in mass effect. With respect to details and accessories, however, the German churches are graced with much that one would gladly find every-where as an expression of the artistic embellishment of a great religious edifice.

In spite of the austerity of many of these German churches in the fabric itself, there is frequently an abounding wealth of accessory detail in fitments and fur-nishings.

In France the Revolution made away with much decorative embellishment and furniture of all sorts. The Reformation in Germany played no such part, and so there is left much really artistic detail which contributes a luxuriance that is wanting in constructive details.

The universally elaborate carven pulpits and choir-stalls are wonders of their kind. It is true they are usually of wood instead of stone, but it must be remem-bered that the Germans were ever great wood-workers.

The pulpits of Freiburg and Strasburg are thoroughly representative of the best work of this kind. They may be said, moreover, to be of the Gothic species only, whereas similar works elsewhere are most frequently of the Renaissance pe-riod.

In no other European country are the altars so rich in detail, the sacristies so full to overflowing with jewelled and precious metal cups, vases, and chalices, or the crucifixes, triptychs, and candlesticks so sumptuous.

In the cathedral at Aix-la-Chapelle the congregation seats itself upon chairs; but most frequently in Germany one finds sturdy, though movable, oaken bench-es.

Of the carved choir-stalls, those at St. Géréon's at Cologne are the most nearly perfect of their kind on the Rhine; those at Mayence, while elaborately produced, being of a classic order which is manifestly pagan and out of keeping in a Christian church.

German churches in general made much of the cloister, though not all of the examples that formerly existed have come down to us undisturbed or even in fragmentary condition. But, in spite of the Protestant succession to many of the noble minsters, many of these cloisters have endured in a fair state of preservation. Attached to the western end of St. Maria in Capitola at Cologne is an admirable example, while the Romanesque types at Bonn, at the abbey of Laach, and at Essen are truly beautiful. Examples of the later pure Gothic construction are those at Aix-la-Chapelle and Trèves.

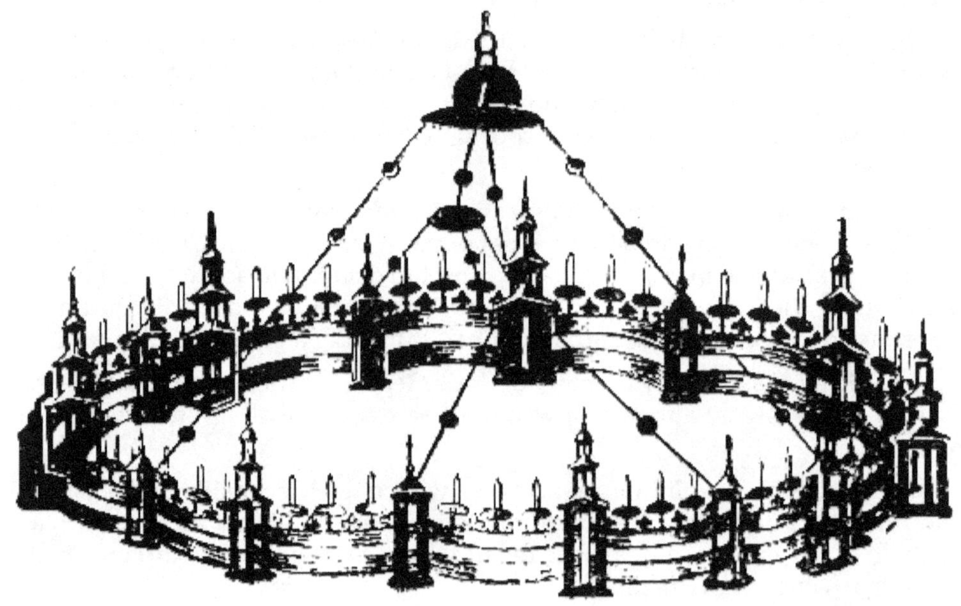

CHANDELIER, AIX-LA-CHAPELLE

But little exterior sculpture has been preserved in all its originality in the Rhenish provinces, revolutionary fury and its aftermath having accounted for its disappearance or mutilation. In the Cistercian church at the abbey of Altenburg, there is a plentiful display of foliaged ornament, and there are the noble statues in the choir of the cathedral at Cologne. Mayence has a series of monuments to the bishop-nobles attached to the piers of the nave, and in the Liebfrau Kirche at Trèves and the cathedral at Strasburg are seen the best and most numerous features of this nature.

One of the most unusual of mediæval church furnishings, a sort of chandelier, is seen both at Aix-la-Chapelle and Hildesheim. In each instance it is a vast hoop-like pendant which bears the definition of *coronæ lucis*. Others are found elsewhere in Germany, but not of the great size of these two.

Organ-cases here as elsewhere are mostly abominations. The makers of sweet music evidently thought that any heavy baroque combination of wood-carving and leaden pipes was good enough so long as the flow of melody was uninterrupted.

The stained glass throughout the Rhine valley is mostly good and unusually abundant, and the freedom of this accessory from fanatical desecration is most apparent. The same is true of such paintings as are found hung in the churches, though seldom have they great names attached to them; at least, not so great as would mark them for distinction were they hung in any of the leading picture galleries of Europe.

At Essen the baptistery is separated from the main church, like that at Ravenna, or at Aix-en-Provence, the two foremost examples of their kind. A little to the westward of this minster, and joined to it by a Romanesque ligature, is a three-bayed Gothic church which occupies the site, or was built up from a former chapel dedicated to St. John the Baptist.

FONT, LIMBURG

Sooner or later the custom became prevalent of erecting a baptismal font within the precincts of the main church itself, thus doing away with a structure especially devoted to the purpose. This change came in the ninth century, hence no separate baptisteries are found dating from a later epoch only, except as an avowed copy of the earlier custom.

At this time, too, immersion had given way to sprinkling merely, though in many cases the German name still applied is that of *taufstein*, meaning dipping-stone.

Late examples of fonts were frequently in metal, the most remarkable in the Rhine valley being in St. Reinhold's at Dortmund, in St. Maria in Capitola, and St. Peter's at Cologne, and in St. Mary's and St. James's at Mayence.

One of the most elaborate, and certainly the most beautiful and remarkable of all, is the stone font of the cathedral at Limburg.

CHAPTER VI
CONSTANCE AND SCHAFFHAUSEN

Constance

THERE is a sentimental interest attached to Constance and the lake which lies at its door, which has come down to us through the pictures of the painters and the verses of the poets. Aside from this, history has played its great part so vividly that one could not forget it if he would.

The city was founded about 297 A.D. In after years it fell before the warlike Huns, and all but disappeared, until it became the seat of a bishop in the sixth century, the jurisdiction of the bishopric extending for a dozen leagues in all directions.

In the tenth century it became a *ville impériale,* and by the fifteenth it had a population of more than forty thousand souls, and the bishopric counted eight hundred thousand adherents. To-day the city proper has decreased in numbers to a population which hovers closely about the five thousand mark.

The emperors convoked many Diets at Constance, and in 1183 the peace was signed here between the Emperor Barbarossa and the Lombard towns.

The cathedral, or münster, of Constance is dedicated to "Our Lady", and is for the most part a highly satisfying example of a Renaissance church, though here and there may be noticed the Gothic, which was erected on the eleventh-century foundations.

The façade has been restored in recent years, and is flanked by two pseudo-Romanesque towers or campaniles in the worst of taste.

The interior is divided into three naves by columns bearing rounded arches. Above, in the grand nave, are a series of round-headed windows, while those in the aisles are ogival.

The choir contains a series of Gothic stalls in stone, which, unless it has very recently been scraped off, are covered with the ordinary cheap whitewash.

The painted vaulting is atrocious, and, while its hideous colouring lasts, it matters little whether it is of the Romanesque barrel style or ogival. The nervures are there, so it must belong to the latter variety, but it is all so thickly covered with what looks like enamel paint and gaudy red and blue "lining" that it is painful to contemplate.

CONSTANCE CATHEDRAL

There is a fine statue of John Huss supporting the pulpit. It is an adequate monument to one who made history so vivid that it reads almost like legend. In the pavement is a *plaque* of copper which indicates the spot where Huss stood when his sentence was read out to him. According to tradition—some have said that it was the ecclesiastical law—Huss was hurled from the church by a *coup de pied*.

The organ-case, of the fifteenth century, which backs up the inside wall of the façade, is one of the most gorgeous of its kind extant, although there is no very high art expression to be discovered in the overpowering mass of mahogany and lead pipes which, with inadequate supports, hangs perilously upon a wall.

This particular organ-case is richly sculptured with foliage and figures of men, demons, and what not. If it is symbolic, it is hard to trace the connection between any religious motive and the actual appearance of this ungainly mass of carved wood.

There is in the cathedral an elaborate allegorical painting by Christopher Storer, a native of Constance, and executed in 1659 by the order of Canon Sigismund Müller, who died in 1686, and whose tomb is placed near by.

An immense retable is placed at the head of the nave. It is of fine marble, and, though a seventeenth-century copy of Renaissance, is far more beautiful than such ornaments usually are outside of Italy.

At the head of the left aisle is a chapel which also has an elaborate marble retable of the same period. At the summit is a crucifix, and below in niches are statues of St. Thomas, of Constantine, and of his mother, Ste. Hélène. In the same chapel is a "Christ in the tomb", in marble, surrounded by the twelve apostles.

From the same aisle ascends a charming ogival staircase ornamented with statues and bas-reliefs. Separating the chapels from the aisles are two magnificent iron grilles. In a Gothic chapel near the entrance is a fine *cul de lampe* sculptured to represent the history of Adam and Eve.

A cloister exists, in part to-day as it did of yore, to the northeast of the cathedral. It is a highly beautiful example of fifteenth-century work, with its arcades varying from the firm and dignified early Gothic to the more flamboyant style of later years.

The church of St. Stephen is another ecclesiastical treasure of Constance with a rank high among religious shrines.

St. Stephen's occupies the site formerly given to a chapel dedicated to St. Nicholas, while not far away there was, in other times, another known under the name of Maria Unter der Linden. The Bishop Salomon III., who occupied the see from 891 to 919, enlarged the first chapel, which was further embellished in 935 by the Bishop Conrad of Altdorf, who added a choir thereto.

This in time came to be known as St. Stephen's. It was entirely renovated in 1047-51 by the Bishop Theodoric, who was interred therein upon his death. The church served as the meeting-place of the famous Roman tribunal known as the *Sacra Rota Romana*. Under the Bishop Otto III., who was Margrave of Hochberg, it was entirely reconstructed in 1428, and to-day it is this fifteenth-century building that one sees. Previously, if the records tell truly, the great windows of the clerestory contained coloured glass of much beauty, but the remains of to-day are so fragmentary as to only suggest this.

From 1522 to 1548 St. Stephen's was consecrated to the followers of Luther, the first incumbent under this belief being the famous Jacob Windner of Reutlingen.

The exterior of St. Stephen's is not in any way remarkable. The bell-tower, which is very high, is a great square tower to the left of the choir, surmounted by a steeple formerly covered with wooden shingles, but in recent times coppered. The clock in this tower was the gift of Bishop Otto III. There is also a fine chime of bells, which will remind one of the churches of the Low Countries when he hears its limpid notes ring out upon the still air.

The interior has been newly whitened with that peculiar local brand of whitewash, and while bright and cheerful to contemplate, is also very bare, caused perhaps by the vast size of the nave and choir.

The aisles are separated from the nave by ogival arches, rising from a series of octagonal pillars, upon which are hung statues of the twelve apostles. The wooden roof of the nave and its aisles is curious and dates from 1600, but it is mostly hidden by a plaster covering which was added in the early nineteenth century.

The gilded and highly decorated organ and its case dates from 1583. In 1819 and 1839 it was "restored," whatever that may mean with regard to an organ, and at some time between the two dates were added two colossal figures of David and St. Cecilia. There are numerous and elaborate paintings in St. Stephen's which would make many more popular shrines famous. The most notable are "St. John before King Wenceslas," "The Stoning of St. Stephen," "The Glory of the Lamb," and an "Adoration," the work of Philip Memberger, who painted this last at the time of the reëstablishment of the Catholic faith at Constance in 1550. A portrait of the artist is preserved in the sacristy.

Many other works of art were demolished or carried away in the years of the Reformation.

In 1414 three Popes disputed the honour of occupying the Holy See, John XXIII., Gregory XII., and Benoit XIII. The Emperor Sigismund, after having met the deputies of each of the aspirants at Como and Lodi, assembled a council to put an end, if possible, to the anarchy which had arisen within the Church. Its place of meeting was Constance, and the emperors, kings, princes, cities, churches, and universities of Germany, Sweden, Denmark, Hungary, Bohemia, and Italy all sent their deputations. France was represented by Pierre d'Ailly, Archbishop of Cambrai, and Jean Gerson, the chancellor of the University of Paris.

The Council of Constance was the most numerous body which had ever been called together on behalf of the Church. It opened its sessions on the 5th of November, 1414, and continued until the 12th of April, 1418.

John XXIII. declared that he would abdicate if his two competitors would agree to follow his example. Gregory XII. agreed to this and sent his abdication to the council by an ambassador, Carlo Malatesta; but Benoit XIII. fled to Spain and still clung tenaciously to the title of Pope. Finally, at a conclave composed of thirty-two cardinals, Othon Colonna was, in 1417, elected Pope under the name of Martin V.

The council held at Constance which condemned John Huss, who was a Wyclif disciple before he was one of Luther's, took place in 1414. Huss was condemned to be burned alive in 1415, and "he mounted the pile," says history, "with the courage of a martyr."

One may see in the Place Brühl, a kilometre from the centre of Constance, the very spot where the "pile" was erected.

The present customs warehouse (Kaufhaus) formed Constance's famous council-chamber, and to-day it is one of the most interesting curiosities of the city.

The grand council-chamber is situated on the first floor of the building, and was erected in 1388. Its length approximates two hundred feet, and it is perhaps one hundred in width with a height of twenty feet.

The ceiling is held aloft by fourteen wooden pillars, and there are twenty-three windows.

There are no traces of wall decorations, and the opinion is hazarded that the walls and pillars were, at the time of the council, hung with draperies.

From the windows there is a fine view of the Lake of Constance, and but a little distance away is the Franciscan convent, now transformed into a factory, where was incarcerated John Huss previous to his martyrdom.

Schaffhausen

Of the falls of Schaffhausen, Victor Hugo wrote: "*Effroyable tumulte.*" This is the first impression. The four grand, overflowing channels of the cataract tumble, rise and redescend in an eternal tempest of rage.

A musical German once said that the only way to express the tumult of Schaffhausen's fall was to "put it to music." He probably had Wagner in mind, and perhaps there are persons who could conjure up a picture of its foam-decked course by means of the master's harmonies.

Montaigne was of a more practical turn of mind. He said: "*Cela arrête le cours des bateaux et interrompt la navigation de ladite rivière.*"

Compared with Niagara, Victoria Nyanza, or the great cataract at Yosemite, the falls of Schaffhausen depict no great splendour of aspect, though they are tumultuous and unqualifiedly picturesque. Furthermore, they form a pretty setting for the little city of some five thousand souls which bears the same name.

With Basel, Schaffhausen has preserved its mediæval character far more than the other cities of Switzerland. Its streets are narrow and irregular, and most of its houses are of the deep-gabled variety, many of them having their fronts frescoed in truly theatrical fashion, the effect, as might be supposed, being highly pleasing.

Schaffhausen owes its prominence in the commercial world to its falls, which make it necessary for merchandise making its way between Constance and the Lower Rhine to be transshipped at this point. The traffic is by no means so large as that which goes on in the Lower Rhine, but it does exist in proportions so considerable as to justify a certain activity in this old-world town which is noticeable to-day, and which has existed for many centuries. The name Schaffhausen (Schiff-hausen) comes, it is claimed, from the houses of the boatmen, and this seems sufficiently plausible to be accepted without question.

The Fortress of Munoth dominates the city, crowning the height of Mont Emmers. It occupies the site of an ancient Roman stronghold, and, like its fellows which crown the heights bordering upon the German Rhine, is formidable in its grimness if not for its actual value in modern warfare.

In 1052, Count Eberhardt of Nellenburg founded an abbey here, and accorded to the abbot rights and powers without limitation, so far as the count's seigneurial lands were concerned. To-day, however, Schaffhausen is not rich in ecclesiastical monuments. Its cathedral is a Byzantine edifice of the twelfth century, and is a development from the church of the ancient abbey founded by Count Eberhardt.

There are no constructive or decorative details which call for remark, save twelve columns, each cut from a solid block of sandstone. They measure perhaps twenty feet in height, and are three feet or more in circumference.

There is no resemblance between the architecture of this church and others in the Rhine valley; therefore it cannot be considered as typical of any Rhenish manner of building.

St. John's is an ogival edifice also without any great merit, unless it be that of a grandeur which is contrastingly out of place in its cramped surroundings.

Below Schaffhausen is Sackingen, the third forest city of the Rhine. It owes its origin to a convent of St. Hilaire, founded in the sixth century by St. Fridolin.

The "Lives of the Saints" recounts how St. Columba and his disciples left Ireland and came to Constance, where they separated and went their various ways to evangelize the Rhine valley. To St. Fridolin fell that part lying between Basel and Laufenburg. His bones are yet venerated in the church of St. Hilaire.

COAT OF ARMS, CONSTANCE

CHAPTER VII
BASEL AND COLMAR

Basel

AFTER traversing several of the Swiss cantons, the Rhine leaves Switzerland at Basel. After the breaking up of the vast empire of Charlemagne, Basel came first under the authority of the Emperors of Germany, and then under that of the kings of the second house of Burgundy, until 1032, at which time the city became definitely incorporated into the German Empire.

Rudolph of Hapsburg besieged the city in 1274, and through the fourteenth and well into the fifteenth century it was the theatre of many struggles between the bishops and the emperors.

In 1061 and 1431 important councils of the Church were held here.

In 1489, at the village of Dornach, scarce half a dozen miles from Basel, took place that battle between six thousand Swiss and fifteen thousand Austrians which made possible the future independence of Switzerland.

During the sixteenth century Basel enjoyed a glorious era with respect to science and art.

Its university, the oldest in Switzerland, founded by Pius II., shone brilliantly with the reflected light of the philosopher Erasmus, the alchemist Paracelsus, and many theologians and geographers. Hans Holbein was born here in the seventeenth century.

The Rhine divides the city into two unequal parts, which are connected by a bridge which was originally constructed in 1220.

Although Basel bears even yet, in its architecture, the stamp of an imperial city of the middle ages, it must be counted as somewhat modern. Nevertheless, of all the cities of the first rank in Switzerland it resisted the march of innovation the longest. For instance, there was a time when all the clocks of the city were an hour behind those of their neighbours. In 1778, however, the Swiss government decreed that on the first of the following January all the clocks of the city must be regulated by solar time. The innovation excited the indignation of the people exceedingly; but, fifteen days after the date originally set, the city fell in with the new regulation, and took up anew the routine of its life.

CATHEDRAL CLOCK, BASEL

"The most magnificent of the Swiss women," says a gallant French writer, "are those of Basel, but they know too much (at all times and all places)," he continued, somewhat dulling the effect of his praises.

"They have an elegance of carriage and dress, which, added to their naturally agreeable qualities, gives them a preëminence over all other women of Switzerland."

All this is as flowery a compliment as the fair sex of any country could receive, and, judging from appearances, as one lingers a few hours or a few days in Basel, it is all true.

The most remarkable of all the edifices of Basel is its cathedral, or münster, dedicated to the Virgin.

BASEL AND ITS CATHEDRAL

In certain of its features one finds a distinct Lombard influence,—in its sculptures and carvings, notably the two carved lions in the crypt, which are the counterparts of others at Modena and Verona in Italy,—though in general it is a Gothic structure.

The cathedral was founded by the Emperor Henry II. of Bavaria in 1010, and was dedicated in 1019.

It is constructed of red sandstone, as are the chief of the architectural monuments along the Rhine, and is an imposing example of the Gothic of that time.

The great portal on the west is richly decorated in the archivolt. It is flanked on either side by an arcade whose buttress pillars are each surmounted by a statue in a canopied niche or *baldaquin*.

At the foot of the north tower is an equestrian statue of St. George and the Dragon, and at the angle of the southern tower is another of St. Martin.

Two small doorways, each entering the side aisles, flank the arcade of the portal. Above the principal doorway of this façade is a *balcon à jour* before the great window which lights the main nave.

The towers rise beside this great window, and are of themselves perhaps the most remarkable features of the church.

They are not exactly alike, but they reflect more than any other part of the edifice the characteristics of the Gothic of these parts. The northern tower was completed in 1500, and is sixty-six metres in height. The southern tower is perhaps more ornate, and resembles, if somewhat faintly, Texier's beautiful spire at Chartres.

The ogival windows of the side walls are strong and of ample proportions.

At the extremity of the north transept is a doorway known as the Porte de St. Gall, decorated with statues of the four evangelists. Above is a great round window of the variety so commonly seen in France. It is here known as the "Wheel of Fortune." It is not a particularly graceful design, the rays or spokes being formed of tiny *colonnettes*, but is interesting nevertheless and quite unusual along the Rhine.

The coping of the roof of the nave is formed of party-coloured tiles, which give it a singular bizarre effect when viewed from near by.

The interior divides itself in the conventional manner into three naves, which are bare and with no ornamentation whatever.

The pulpit is a real work of art, and there are some sculptured capitals in the choir which are quite excellent.

The baptismal fonts are elaborately carved. One of these, bearing the date of 1465, is shaped something like a gigantic egg-cup. Its bowl springs from the stem in eight facets, sculptured to illustrate the baptism of Christ in the waters of the Jordan, with figures of St. Lawrence, St. Jacques, St. Paul, St. Pierre, and St. Martin.

Holbein once made a series of decorations for the organ-case of this church, but they exist no longer.

Beneath the edifice, with its entrance from the choir, is a crypt nearly as large as the nave itself, with a series of massive pillars supporting its vault and the pavement of the church proper.

There are numerous monuments within the church, including one to Erasmus, the illustrious Hollander who had made Basel his second home.

A stairway leads from the church to the chamber where was held, from 1431 to 1444, the famous Council of Basel. It is a vast, bare room, with no furniture whatever, except the benches upon which sat the prelates assembled at the council.

The cloister attached to the cathedral is daintily planned and contains a number of tombs of celebrated persons.

Behind the church is a magnificent terrace known as the Pfalz. It is planted with chestnut-trees, and its elevation, high above the level of the Rhine waters, makes it a magnificent promenade.

The Hôtel of the Three Kings—though it is to-day a modern structure that one sees—was, in the ninth century, the meeting-place of Conrad III., Henry III., and Rudolph III., the last King of Burgundy. Following another tradition, the house derived its nomenclature from the *reliques* of "the Three Magi," which were lodged here when on their journey, in 1161, from Milan to Cologne.

In the museum at Basel are two of Holbein's, sketches made from statues in the Sainte Chapelle at Bourges in France. They represent the Duke Jean de Berry and his wife, Jeanne de Boulogne. It seems rather curious that a great draughtsman like Holbein should deliberately have set himself to copying from a cast, which is practically what it amounted to in this case, charming though these drawings be.

Colmar

Colmar, the chief town of the "circle of Colmar," was once strongly fortified. It still has something more than fragments left of its seven towered and turreted gates.

Formerly it was the capital of Upper Alsace, and later it was the capital of the Département du Haut-Rhin. As a result of the war of 1871 it became a German city.

To Americans and Frenchmen it will perhaps be most revered as being the birthplace of Auguste Bartholdi, the designer of the celebrated Statue of Liberty at New York. (There is a smaller counterpart at Paris, on the Ile des Cygnes in the Seine, which is often overlooked by visitors to the capital.)

The church of St. Martin is a thirteenth-century Gothic church of more than usual splendour. Its fine foundations date from 1237, and its choir from 1315. It is of the conventional Latin cross form, with two imposing towers and a really grand portal. It is built of red sandstone, and is surmounted with a wonderfully massive steeple, which looks more like an adjunct to a fortification than a dependency of a Christian edifice. There is a counterpart of this feature in the cathedral at Dol in Brittany, but there it has the added detail of a crenelated parapet, which gives it a still more military air.

In other days this great tower on St. Martin's at Colmar served the purposes of a civic belfry as well as that of a Christian campanile.

In the sacristy of this rather grim church is an admirable fifteenth-century work of art, a Virgin surrounded by garlands of roses, executed by Schöngauer, a native of Colmar (1450-88) and one of the greatest painters and sculptors of the fifteenth century.

There is the restored fabric of the famous convent of the Dominicans, known as Unterlinden, which is to be considered as one of the chief curiosities of the town. It was built in 1232, before even the church of St. Martin, and its history was exceedingly prominent in the records of mysticism in Germany.

The conventual establishment was suppressed at the time of the Revolution, but in the mid-nineteenth century it was rebuilt with a great deal of thought for the reproduction of the Gothic architecture of the era of its inception.

COAT OF ARMS, BASEL

CHAPTER VIII

FREIBURG

THE steeple of Freiburg is quite the rival of that of Strasburg; some even may think it more beautiful.

It has braved with impunity the winds and tempests of many centuries, and stands to-day as beautiful a work of its kind, when one is away from Strasburg, Chartres, Antwerp, or Malines, as one can well conceive.

Its appearance is indeed magnificent, with a richness of ornament which has not been carried to the excess that would make it tawdry, and an outline which in every proportion is just and true.

Each day brings new admirers to this shrine, and one and all, antiquarians and cursory travellers alike, go away with an enthusiastic regard for its charms.

Freiburg itself does not go very far back into antiquity. It owes its origin to Berthold III., Duke of Zähringen, who founded it in 1118 and made it the capital of Breisgau, one of the most fertile districts of the ancient German duchy.

The cathedral at Freiburg marks the opening of a new era in the Christian architecture of Germany. It was founded in 1122 by the Duke of Zähringen, soon after he took over the guardianship of the city, but it was only in 1513 that it was entirely completed.

Nothing now remains of the primitive church except the transept and the base of the lateral portals. The nave dates from the middle of the thirteenth century, and the choir was mostly rebuilt at the same time. The dedication did not take place until a century and a half later.

The structure is in the conventional form of a Latin cross, with the usual nave and aisles and a series of chapels surrounding the apside.

The façade is remarkable for the porch, which is highly ornamented with sculpture and forms the lowest story of the tower.

The pediment above the entrance is garnished with statuary representing the crowning of the Holy Virgin, while just below, at the sides, are two kneeling figures, with crowns on their heads, bent in prayer.

Besides this gallery of saintly figures, there are also sculptured symbols which, in such a company, might well be thought profane: figures representing Geometry, Music, Arithmetic, and the Arts.

FREIBURG CATHEDRAL

In the tower, above the porch, is a chapel dedicated to St. Michael, lighted by three ogival windows. It is now a bare, uninteresting chamber, its altar and decorations having disappeared.

The third story of the tower forms the belfry, from which springs the gently tapering and beautiful spire which rises to a height only forty feet less than that of Strasburg.

The dwindling spire has a dozen facets which in some mysterious way unite with the octagon of the belfry in a manner that leaves nothing to criticize.

Within the cathedral there are some acceptable mural decorations in the wall space above the western arch of the transept crossing. There are also a number of funeral monuments, finely sculptured and quite remarkable of their kind. One, a "Christ in the Sepulchre," is admirably executed in the sixteenth-century style of Koempf, who is responsible also for the elaborate pulpit.

There are two other churches in Freiburg of more than usual interest; the parish church with a fine fourteenth-century cloister, and the Protestant temple, a modern structure in the Byzantine style, which has been built up on the remains of the church belonging to the ancient Benedictine convent of Tönnenbach, which existed in the twelfth century.

In the chapel of the university are a number of paintings by Holbein.

COAT OF ARMS, FREIBURG

CHAPTER IX

STRASBURG

The greatest curiosity of Strasburg is the Rhine; after that, its cathedral.

Usually, on entering Strasburg, the first landmark that greets one's eye is the slim, lone spire of the cathedral.

Years ago an itinerant showman travelled about with a model of the celebrated Strasburg clock, and the writer got his first ideas of a great Continental cathedral from the rather crude representation of the Gothic beauties of that at Strasburg, which graced the canvas which hung before the showman's tent.

The clock is still there, in all its mystical incongruity, but one's interest centres in the grace and elegance of the dwindling spire and its substructure of nave, transept, and choir, which dominates all else round about.

Of many eras, the structure of this great Latin-cross cathedral is not harmonious; but, for all that, it is a great Gothic triumph, and one which might well lend most of its details of construction and decoration to any great church, and still add a charm which was hitherto absent.

Strasburg has in all fifteen churches, but the cathedral is possessed of more and greater glories than all the others combined.

From the days when Strasburg was the Argentoratum of the Romans, the city has ever been the scene of an activity which has made its importance known through all the world. It was sacked by Attila and his Huns in 451, and was completely abandoned up to the seventh century, when one of the sons of Clovis built it up anew and gave to it the name of Strateburgum.

Ptolemy is said to be the first writer who mentions Argentoratum, the ancient Strasburg.

What a bitter blow the loss of Alsace-Lorraine, of which Strasburg was the gem, was to France can only be realized by a contemplation of the sentiment which even yet attaches to the event.

That the allied provinces were French in spirit as well as Catholic in religion is demonstrated by the fact that, at the time of the German occupation, there was a population of over a million and a half of souls, of which quite a million and a quarter were of the Roman Catholic faith. About a million and a quarter were natives of Alsace-Lorraine, one hundred thousand were Germans, and thirty odd thousand were foreigners.

The present cathedral was erected on a site that had been consecrated to religion in very early times. It had been a sacred place in the time of the Romans, though the deities worshipped were pagan, a temple to Hercules and Mars having been erected here.

The first Christian church was built, it is believed, in the fifth century, by St. Amand, then Bishop of Strasburg.

This first church of Strasburg, which was a wooden structure, was probably founded by Clovis, 504, and reconstructed by Pepin-le-Bref and Charlemagne. It was mostly destroyed by fire in 873, and in 1002 was pillaged and fired anew by the soldiers of Duke Hermann, who was condemned himself to repair the damage. Lightning destroyed it again in 1007, and, by the time the new structure was thought of, nothing but the crypt of Charlemagne's edifice was visible.

From the proceeds received from Duke Hermann, and contributions from all Christianity, Bishop Werner conceived a vast scheme of a new church which in time was completed and consecrated.

This in turn fell before the ravages of fire, and nothing but a mass of débris remained, from which the present structure was begun in 1277.

The ancient church foundation of Strasburg was peculiarly arranged, after a manner most unusual in a cathedral church. The ground-plan of the ecclesiastical establishment was not unlike those of the monkish communities which were so plentifully scattered over Europe, but it was built for use as a church, and for the bishop and his clerics, instead of being merely a secular monastery.

The following diagram explains this unusual arrangement.

The masonic theory with regard to the construction of these mediæval ecclesiastical monuments is of much interest in connection with Strasburg. The lodge at Strasburg was the earliest in the north of which we have any knowledge, and Ervin von Steinbach himself seems to have been at the head of it, which fact proves that he was one of the first of secular architects engaged upon a great religious work.

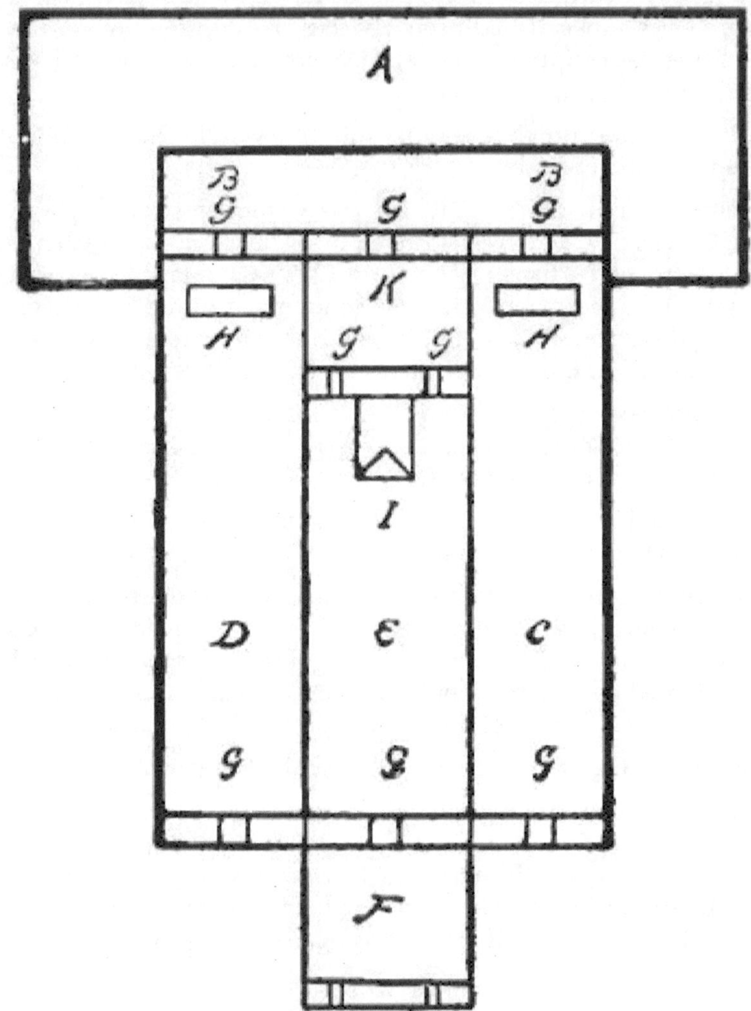

ANCIENT CHURCH FOUNDATION, STRASBURG

A—Habitation of bishops and clerics
B—Cour commune
C—Part assigned to women
D—Part assigned to men
E—For preaching
F—For penitents
G—Doors
H—Altars
I—Pulpits
K—Choir for clergy

Great opportunities and privileges were conferred upon him by Rudolph of Hapsburg, and the masonic lodge of which he was the head had the power, over a wide extent of territory, to maintain order and obedience among the workmen under its jurisdiction.

In 1278 Pope Nicholas III. issued a bull, giving the body absolution, and this was renewed by his successors up to the time of Benedict XII.

STRASBURG CATHEDRAL

Iodoque Dotzinger, master of the works at Strasburg in 1452, formed an alliance between the different lodges of Germany.

It was an appreciative Frenchman—and all Frenchmen are appreciative and fond of Strasburg, because of what it once was to them—that said: "*La cathédrale est un merveille unique au monde.*" Continuing, he said: "Those who have not seen it know not the *gaieté lumineuse* of a Gothic church."

All of this is of course quite true from some points of view.

There is, however, something pitiful about the general aspect of this great Gothic church. Its lone spire, standing grim and gaunt against a background of sky, makes only the more apparent the incompleteness of the structure.

Its façade is certainly marvellous, quite rivalling those of Reims and Toul, not so very far away across the French border.

The triple porch of the façade is rich in sculpture, the most remarkable groups being "The Wise and Foolish Virgins," "The Prophets," "The Last Judgment," and "Christ and the Twelve Apostles."

A great rose window, a reminiscence of the masterpieces so frequently seen in France, also decorates this elaborate façade.

The south portal is in the form of two round-arched doorways, and is a survival, evidently, of one of the earliest epochs of this style of construction. It is ornamented with bas-reliefs and statues symbolical of the triumph of Christian religion. There has recently been erected before this portal a statue of the great architect of the fabric, Ervin, and another of his son.

The spire, one of the most elevated in Europe, is 440 feet, while that of Cologne is 482 feet, Rouen is 458 feet, and Notre Dame at Paris but 200 feet in height.

Usually church edifices are grim and gray; but Strasburg presents, in its sandstone of the Vosges, a beautiful tone, which in the westering sun of a summer's day can only be described as a rose-pink, and is like no other church edifice in Europe, unless it be the cathedral at Rodez in Mid-France, which Henry James called mouse-coloured, but which in reality is a sort of warm, deep rose.

A fine lacework of *colonnettes* covers the entire façade, which six centuries have turned to the colour of iridescent copper organ-pipes.

But the real grandeur and dignity of the architecture stands out boldly in spite of the ornate turrets and the mass of sculptured detail, in a way which stamps the fabric imperially as a giant among its kind.

Of the spire, Victor Hugo wrote thus (Strasburg was yet French, and not German as it is to-day): "The truly adorable achievement of the builders of this cathedral is its spire. It is a tiara of stone crowned with a cross. It is prodigious, gigantic, but of great delicacy. I have seen Chartres; I have seen Antwerp. Four *escaliers à jour* ascend spirally the four towerlets at the angles. The steps are very high and narrow.... To mount to the lantern one would have to follow the workmen, who appear to be continually engaged on the fabric. The stairways are no more, simply bars of iron set ladderlike in the masonry.

"From the spire one sees three mountain ranges: the group of the Black Forest to the north; the Vosges to the west; and the Alps to the south.

"One stands so high that the country-side appears no longer as the country-side; but, like the view from the castle at Heidelberg, a mere geographical map.

"At the time of my visit a great cloud rose up from the valley of the Rhine, and framed the panorama for a dozen leagues in truly eerie fashion. As I went from one tower to another, I saw about me la France, la Suisse, and l'Allemagne."

It was in 1277 that the celebrated architect, Ervin von Steinbach, began the construction of the portal of the cathedral at Strasburg, and above its great doorway one may yet read, if he be keen of eyesight and knows where to look for it, this inscription:

ANNO. DOMINI. MCCLXXVII. IN. DIE.
BEATI.
URBANI. HOC. GLORIOSUM. OPUS.
INCOHAVIT.
MAGISTER. ERVINUS DE STEINBACH.

Ervin died in 1318, and his son continued the work up to the first landing, or platform, of the towers.

In the archives of the cathedral are still to be seen the designs on which father and son worked in achieving the portal and towers, as well as those of the spire, the north porch, the pulpit, and the organ-buffet. Not all of these are contemporary, but the first, at least, are the very drawings which were handled by Maître Ervin and his son in the latter years of the thirteenth century.

The following lines of Longfellow describe the religious fervour of the great architect perhaps more truthfully than could prose.

> ". . . A great master of his craft,
> Ervin von Steinbach; but not he alone,
> For many generations laboured with him,
> Children that came to see these saints in stone,
> As day by day out of the blocks they rose,
> Grew old and died, and still the work went on,
> And on and on and is not yet completed.

> ". . . The architect
> Built his great heart into these sculptured stones,
> And with him toiled his children, and their lives
> Were builded with his own into the walls
> As offerings to God."

It is perhaps not possible to write of Strasburg's cathedral without giving its great clock more than a passing thought.

The legendary history of the clock at Strasburg is as follows:

The cathedral being terminated, the magistrates of the city desired to ornament its tower with a great clock which should be unique in all the world.

No one came forth to undertake the commission, until a workman, much advanced in years, agreed for a certain sum to produce a clock which should be superior to all others then existing.

After some years of incessant work, he produced the first of Strasburg's wonderful mechanical clocks full of moving figures and symbols.

In lieu of recompense, the magistrates, desiring that their city should be the sole possessor of such a work, accused the old man of having had resource to the aid of the devil in producing so weird a timepiece, and condemned him to torture and the loss of his eyesight.

Upon a pretext of making some further arrangement of the works before the execution of his sentence, the old man was allowed once more to mount the tower. Instead of adjusting the clock, he deranged it in some way so that its chimes never rang out as intended, and thus the magistrates and the citizens of Strasburg were, in a way, avenged for the injustice done the inventor. This famous clock of Strasburg's tower is now only a memory.

The more recent works of a similar nature have a history less sordid and unpleasant. The first clock of the cathedral, placed inside the church at the crossing, dated from 1352, and of course was a remarkable work for its time.

Two hundred years later it was intended to replace it with another, but the work was never achieved, so a third was begun with an effort to outdo the ingenuity which had made possible the fourteenth-century astronomical wonder.

It was planned in 1571, under the direction of Conrad Dasypodius, of Strasburg, and his friend Daniel Volkenstein, an astronomer of Augsburg. It was completed in 1574, restored in 1669 and 1732, and ceased its labours through the stress of time in 1790.

The present great clock, certainly an unseemly and incongruous adjunct of a great church, was commenced on the 24th of June, 1838, and installed on the 31st of December, 1842. Its construction is supposed to have reflected great credit upon its designer, one Schwilgu, a clock-maker of Strasburg. Nothing was preserved of the more ancient timepiece, except its elaborate case, which was restored and further embellished.

At the base of the tower, on the summit of which is placed the crowing cock, is a portrait of the designer. "This great man," say the local patriots, died an octogenarian in 1856.

In 1723 a subterranean tremor sent the tower of Strasburg's cathedral a foot out of plumb. It speaks well for the solidity of the construction that no ill effects resulted, and to-day there are no evidences, to the casual observer, of this deflection.

The beauty of Strasburg's cathedral was in so great repute in the middle ages that Jean Galeaz Marie, Visconti Sforza, in 1481, demanded of the magistrates of the city the name of an architect capable of completing his cathedral at Milan.

In a vaulted chamber attached to the cathedral proper are two strangely curious memorials. They are nothing more or less than two mummies which, for their better preservation, have been varnished, and the costumes which they anciently wore have from time to time been renewed.

One is the mummy of the Count of Nassau-Saarbruck, who died in the sixteenth century, and the other is that of a young girl of perhaps twenty years, supposed to have been his daughter.

The ancient church of St. Bartholomew is another of Strasburg's ecclesiastical shrines which ranks high among great churches.

It dates from the second half of the thirteenth century, but frequent additions have been made in more recent times.

It possesses a remarkable monument which shows a painted "Danse des Morts," with figures of nearly life size. It is a fresco on the inner walls of the overhanging canopy of a tomb. The painting dates from the fifteenth century, but was only discovered in 1824, on the occasion of a general renovation of the church.

The choir was begun in 1308 and completed in 1345. Its height and its general airiness, and the lightness of its vaulting and arches, unite in making it quite unusual and most worthy of note.

This ancient church to-day is occupied by the Protestants, and the edifice has been divided up in a somewhat sacrilegious manner in order to provide within its walls for a library and a museum.

Strasburg has another great church in St. Thomas, a vast ogival edifice which has some good glass, but which is remarkable above all else for the number of its sepulchral monuments, both ancient and modern.

At the end of the choir is found one of those wonders of French sculpture, an allegorical grouping of figures on the tomb of Maréchal de Saxe.

It was erected in 1777 by Pigalle by the order of Louis XV. For a background it has a pyramid of gray marble, at the base of which is the following inscription:

MAVRITIO SAXONI
CVRLANDIAE ET SEMIGALLIAE DVCI
SVMMO REGIORVM EXERCITVVM
PRAEFECTO
SEMPER VICTORI
LVDOVICVS XV
VICTORIARVM AVCTOR ET IPSE DVX
PONI IVSSIT
OBIIT XXX NOV. ANNO MDCCL. AETATIS
LV.

Standing in the centre of the pyramid is a figure of the maréchal descending toward the sarcophagus below. A figure representing Death is lifting the lid, and another, representing France, is endeavouring to stay his hand. Flags, a reversed torch, and other symbols, with another figure representing the genius of war, complete the details of this elaborate monument.

There is little of anything but Gothic, more or less pure, visible at Strasburg;

but, in spite of this, it is alleged that, from Carlovingian times onward, there was here a colony of artisans who had been sent from Lombardy on account of the increased interest in the north in church-building. If this is so, they must have pushed onward down the Rhine, as they left but little impression here, and, while Rhenish church-building was manifestly not Gothic in its inception, here at Strasburg there are certainly no evidences of the Comacine builders of Charlemagne's time.

Strasburg's ancient episcopal palace was built in 1731-41 by Cardinal de Rohan. It was bought by the city before the Revolution and transformed into a *château impérial*, and became later the home of the local university.

The edifice known in early days as the "Maison de l'Oeuvre Notre Dame," and more recently as "Stift zu unser lieben Frauen," was built in 1581, numerous Gothic sculptures from the cathedral being used in its construction. There is here a remarkable spiral staircase in the light and delicate flowered Gothic of its time.

COAT OF ARMS, STRASBURG

CHAPTER X

METZ

From across the Moselle, on the height just to the south of the city of Metz, is to be had one of those widely spread panoramas which defy the artist or the photographer to reproduce.

There is an old French saying that the Rhine had power; the Rhône impetuosity; the Loire nobility; and the Moselle elegance and grace. This last is well shown in the charming river-bottom which spreads itself about the ancient Mediomatricorum, as Metz was known to the Romans.

The enormously tall nave and transepts of the cathedral of Metz dominate every other structure in the city, in a fashion quite in keeping with the strategic importance of the place from a military point of view.

Time was when ecclesiastical affairs and military matters were much more closely allied than now, and certainly if there was any inspiration to be got from a highly impressive religious monument in their midst, the warriors of another day, at Metz, must have felt that they were doubly blessed.

Since the Franco-Prussian war, Metz, with Strasburg, has become transformed; but its ancient monuments still exist to charm and gratify the antiquarian. Indeed, it was as recently as 1900 that the Tour des Lennyers, a wonderful structure of Roman times, was discovered.

Metz was fortified as early as in the third century, and to-day its walls and moats, though modern,—the work of Vauban,—are still wonders of their kind.

In the Roman period the city was of great importance. In the fifth century it was attacked, taken, and destroyed by the Huns; but, when it was rebuilt and became the capital of Austrasia, its prosperity grew rapidly. In 1552 the Due de Montmorenci made himself master of the city, and some months later Henri II. made his *entrée*. During the winter of the same year it successfully resisted Charles V., thanks to François de Lorraine and the Duc de Guise.

The great abbey of St. Arnulphe disappeared at this time. It stood on the site of the present railroad station, where, in 1902, were found many fragments of religious sculptures, coming presumably from the old abbey.

In 1556-62 the citadel was constructed by Maréchal Vielleville. Within the citadel was the old church of St. Pierre, one of those minor works of great beauty which are often overlooked when summing up the treasures of a cathedral town. The old church dated originally from the seventh century, though reconstructed anew in the tenth, and again in the fifteenth century.

METZ

The walls of the surrounding fortifications are of incontestable antiquity. Beneath the pavement of the chapel have recently been found fragments of sculptured stone dating from Merovingian times.

It was during a dangerous illness at Metz that Louis XV. is said to have made the vow which led to the erection of that pagan-looking structure, the church of Sainte Geneviève, more commonly known as the Pantheon, at Paris. It is the largest modern church in France, if, indeed, one can really consider it to-day as a church.

Metz, before its annexation by Germany, was as French as Reims or Troyes. Many of the natives of the city have since left, but they have been replaced by Germans, so the population has not suffered in numbers.

Of a population of forty-five thousand, there are twenty-four thousand soldiers. Hotels, shops, and cafés have become Germanized, but, curiously enough, many, if not nearly all, of the cab-drivers speak French, and French money passes current everywhere.

Certain restaurants preserve what they call the *traditions de la cuisine française*, and in the municipal theatre a company of French players come from Nancy three times a week in the winter season.

Metz, one of the three ancient bishoprics of imperial Lorraine, now forms a part of Elsass-Lothringen, where the German Emperor reigns as emperor and not merely as King of Prussia.

The churches of Metz show very little of Romanesque influences, though it is indeed strong in churches dating from the thirteenth century onward. Early Gothic in nearly every shade of excellence is to be found in the churches of Metz, from the cathedral church of St. Stephen downwards, and, because of this, it is the Continental city where the development of the style can be most thoroughly studied and appreciated.

In many cases there are only fragments, at least, that which is to be admired is more or less fragmentary; but, in spite of that, they are none the less precious and valuable as a record.

Besides its churches, Metz has, in its ancient donjon or castle-keep, a singularly impressive monument of its past greatness, which stands in the *Geisbergstrasse*, or the *Rue de Chèvremont*, as the street is called by the French, for Metz, like Strasburg and the other cities and towns of poor rent Alsace and Lorraine, is even yet a muddle of French and German proper names.

This great pile was doubtless the former royal shelter of Theodoric and others of his line.

To-day Metz is mostly a city of strategic fortifications; but this is but one aspect, and the seat of the renowned bishopric of Lorraine has in its cathedral church an ecclesiastical monument of almost supreme rank.

St. Stephen's Cathedral is a vast structure of quaint and almost grotesque outline, when seen from across the Moselle. Its chief distinction, at first glance, is its height, which seems to dwarf all its other proportions; but in reality it is attenuated in none of its dimensions, and its clerestory is hugely impressive, where one so often finds this feature a mere range of shallow windows.

Among the great churches of Northern Europe, the cathedral of St. Stephen stands third, it being surpassed only by the cathedrals of Beauvais and Cologne.

This fact is frequently overlooked, and ordinarily Metz would be classed with that secondary group which includes Reims, Bourges, and Narbonne; but so accurate an authority as Professor Freeman vouches for the statement.

The clerestory, of a prodigious height, is borne aloft by a series of rather squat-looking pillars, but again figures demonstrate that the cathedral at Metz is truly one of the wonders of its kind.

There is a north tower which is, or was, a part of the civic establishment as well, in that it contained an alarm-bell, similar to those employed in the Netherlands, known as La Mutte. Twin towerlets straddle the nave of the cathedral in a quite unexplainable manner.

Altogether the building has a most remarkable and not wholly beautiful skyline, to which one must become accustomed before it is wholly loved.

Decidedly the least likable portion of the exterior of St. Stephen's is the west front, which is decidedly incongruous, whereas in most places it is the west front that shines and is truly brilliant. Certainly, in this respect Metz does not follow that French tradition which, in its Gothic churches, it otherwise obeys.

St. Stephen's really rises to almost a supreme height. It has been said to exceed that of Amiens and Beauvais, but this is manifestly not so, for, if the figures are correct, it is some seven feet lower than Amiens and twenty lower than Beauvais. Still, it rises to a daring height, and its "walls of glass," with their enormously tall clerestory windows, only accentuate its airiness and grace.

This last quality is remarkable in Gothic architecture of so early a period, the thirteenth century. At St. Ouen at Rouen, to which its openness may be compared, and perhaps to Gloucester in England, the work is of a much later date.

The interior of St. Stephen's presents an equally marked effect of height and brilliancy, with perhaps an exaggeration of the ample clerestory at the expense of the triforium.

There is a remarkable symmetry in the nave and its aisles; and its strong columns, with their shafting rising to the roof groins, show a method of construction so daring that modern builders certainly would not care to copy it.

The glass of the great clerestory windows in the choir dates only from the sixteenth century, and was designed by one Bousch of Strasburg.

The windows of the north and south transepts are exceedingly brilliant specimens of the mediæval glass-workers' art. There are some fragmentary remains, in the clerestory of the nave, of glass of a much earlier period than that in the choir, possibly contemporary with the fabric itself (thirteenth century). If this is so, it is of the utmost value, worthy to be admired with the gold and jewelled treasures of the cathedral's sacristy.

In the sacristy there used to be the ring of Arnulphe and the mantle of Charles the Great, but doubts have been cast upon the latter, and the former has disappeared.

There is, somewhere about the precincts of the cathedral, a weird effigy of a monster known as the *Grauly*, which, like the *Tarasque* at Tarascon and the dragon of St. Bertrand de Comminges, is a made-up, theatrical property which even in its symbolism is ludicrous in its false sentiment.

Besides Metz's cathedral, there is the church of St. Vincent on an island in the river, which lacks orientation and faces almost due south. It is as distinctly a German type of church as the cathedral is French; but this is more as regards its outline than anything else, for its Gothic is very, very good. Its interior is dignified, but graceful, though it lacks a triforium.

St. Martin's is a smaller church, but is contemporary with St. Stephen's and St. Vincent's (thirteenth century).

St. Maximin's is a still smaller edifice, and would be called Romanesque if German did not suit it better. It resembles somewhat the parish churches seen in the country-side in England, and is in no way remarkable or highly interesting, if we except the tall central tower.

St. Eucharius's and St. Sagelone's complete the list of the unattached churches of Metz; St. Clement's being but an attribute of the Jesuit college.

St. Eucharius's stands near what we would call the German Gate,—locally known as Deutsches Thor, or the Porte des Allemands,—a mediæval gateway built into, or built around, rather, by the modern fortifications with which the city is protected.

The church is most lofty for its size. Its pier arches are of great proportions, and its clerestory, like St. Stephen's itself, is of more than ordinarily ample dimensions. There is no triforium.

St. Sagelone's remains practically a pure Gothic example of its time, rather later than the rest of its kind in Metz. It has some fine coloured glass, in spite of the fact that its antiquity cannot be very great.

St. Clement's is a dependency of the Jesuit installation, which reflects more credit upon that order than has usually been accorded them in the arts of church-building.

It is a more or less incongruous combination of the Italian and Gothic styles, but blended with such a consummate skill that the effect can but be admired.

In form St. Clement's is frankly a *Hallenkirche*, with the three naves of equal height. In general the nave is late Gothic, with the marked tracery of its time in its fenestration.

The capitals of the piers, supporting the arches between the nave and its aisles, are stately but heavy, according to Gothic standards, and appear misplaced, luxurious though they undeniably are. St. Clement's is supposed to resemble the variety of Gothic which has been employed in Sicily, where Gothic of the best was known, but was used in conjunction with other details, which really added nothing to its value or beauty as a distinct style.

One leaves Metz with the memory full of visions of many churches and much soldiery of the conventional German type.

There is plenty, in all of these towns, to remind one of both France and Germany. In the geography of other times, Metz was Lotharingian; but French was very early the language of the city, and its prelates and churchmen, when they did not use Latin, spoke only the French tongue, and fell under French influences. Therefore it was but natural that the type of Metz's principal church should have favoured the French style, even though it developed German tendencies.

CHAPTER XI

SPEYER

When Christianity penetrated into the vast and populous provinces of Germany, the Frankish kings favoured its progress and founded upon the banks of the Rhine many religious establishments.

Dagobert I., King of Austrasia, built the first church at Speyer, upon the ruins of a temple which the Romans had consecrated to Diana. When, at the beginning of the eleventh century, this early structure fell in ruins, thanks to the bounty of Conrad II., another of far greater and more beautiful proportions was erected.

The idea of a new edifice was proposed to Walthour, then bishop, who, like many of his fellow prelates of the time, was himself an architect of no mean attainments. The difficult art of church-building had no secrets from the bishop, and he set about the work forthwith, and with ardour. He worked three years upon the plans, and on the 12th of July, 1030, in the presence of the vassals and seigneurs of the court, the emperor laid the foundation-stone of the present cathedral, and declared that the church should serve as the sepulchre of the princes of his race. Twelve tombs were prepared beneath the choir, which itself is known as "the Choir of the Kings," in the same way as the cathedral itself has come to be known as the "Cathedral of the Emperors."

Eight emperors and three empresses have been placed within these tombs: Conrad II., Henry III., Henry IV., Henry V., Philip of Suabia, Rudolph of Hapsburg, Albert of Austria, Adolph of Nassau, the wife of Conrad II., Bertha, the unfortunate companion of Henry IV., and Beatrice, the wife of the great Barbarossa.

Above the tombs of the emperors one may read the following Latin inscription:

> *"Filius hic — Pater Hic — Avus Hic — Proavus jacet istic — Hic proavi conjux — Hic Henrici Senioris."*

The cathedral of Speyer was far from being completed at this time, but the new bishop, Siegfried, was a no less able architect than his predecessor, and he directed the work with zeal and talent.

Already the principal body of the church was rearing itself skyward, and in 1060 the edifice was practically complete, after thirty years of persevering effort.

It is a bizarre sort of a church as seen to-day, and must always have had much the same character; still it is of a style which gave birth to a new and distinct movement in cathedral building, and the authorities have declared that the three edifices founded by the Emperor Conrad, the cathedral of Speyer, the collegiate church of St. Guidon, and the monastery of Limburg, were the foundations of a new school of ecclesiastical architecture, and the envy of all the other provinces of the Empire.

STRASBURG CATHEDRAL

The cathedral was consecrated under Bishop Eginhard, and immediately all church-building Europe went into raptures over it, its proportions and dimensions, its fine plan, its six spires, and the magnificently spacious arrangement of its transept and apside.

In 1159 the fabric suffered much from fire, but before a decade had passed it was restored in such a manner that the church again stood complete.

Another fire followed in 1189, and in 1450 yet another of still greater extent, and only the holy vessels, the reliquaries, and the altar ornaments were saved from the flames.

Bishop Reinhold, of Helmstadt, and the chapter, set about forthwith to rebuild the cathedral, and, while its ashes were still smouldering, they took a vow to make it more beautiful than before.

The bishop wrote a letter to Pope Boniface VIII., on the occasion of his jubilee in the same year, and obtained a pontifical decree that all who gave financial help toward the erection of the new cathedral should be blessed with the same indulgence as those who visited the tombs of the apostles at Rome.

The bishop lost no time, and his agents went forth into all Germany to get funds to reërect the sepulchral church of the emperors. They were received favourably, and twenty-one thousand golden florins furnished Bishop Reinhold the means of carrying out his project.

After the wars of the sixteenth century, when Speyer was sacked, pillaged, and burned, the sturdy walls of the cathedral again fell, and only in the eighteenth century was it restored. For a long time, only the choir was rebuilt, the nave being neglected up to 1772, when Bishop August of Limburg undertook to restore the entire edifice, which, considering that he did it in the eighteenth century, he did comparatively well.

The choir and nave reflect, considerably, the spirit of the middle ages. The façade alone indicates the false taste of the period in which it was restored.

In general the exterior decoration is simple and remarkable for its interest.

The interior was wisely restored in 1823, and shows a series of mural decorations of more than usual excellence, and the statue of Rudolph of Hapsburg, a modern work by a pupil of Thorwaldsen's, is less offensive than might be supposed.

In Speyer's cathedral are an elaborate series of frescoes by Schraudolph, forming a part of the extensive renovation undertaken by Maximilian II. of Bavaria.

The cloister, built in 1437, exists no more. The baptistery is a curious octagonal edifice ornamented with eight columns and surmounted by a dome. It is lighted by eight narrow windows. The origin of the baptistery is in dispute; but, while doubts are likely enough to be cast upon the assertion, it is repeated here, on the strength of the opinion of many authorities, that it may have descended from the time of Dagobert.

There are numerous grotesque carvings, which ornament the cathedral in its various parts, and which have ever been the despair of antiquarians as to their meaning.

In one place on the exterior of the apside is a queerly represented mêlée between gnomish figures of men and beasts with human heads. And again, in the nave, there is a figure of a dwarf with a long beard, with a sort of helmet on his head, and a sword at his side. If he is supposed in any way to represent the Church militant, the symbolism is badly expressed.

St. Bernard preached the Crusades here in the presence of Conrad III., of Hohenstaufen, who was so inspired by the enthusiasm of the holy man that he took the cross himself.

It was in the cathedral of Speyer, too, that St. Bernard added to the canticle of *"Salva Regina"* these words, *"O Clemens! O Pia! O Dulcis Virgo Maria,"* which have since been sung in all the Roman churches of the universe.

An ancient legend recounts how one day St. Bernard had come late to the church, when the statue of the Virgin cried out to him: *"O Bernharde, cur tum tarde?"* and that the saint, with very little respect on this occasion, replied: *"Mulier taceat in ecclesia."* "Since that time," says the legend, "the Madonna has never spoken."

CHAPTER XII

CARLSRUHE, DARMSTADT, AND WIESBADEN

Carlsruhe

CARLSRUHE is modern, very modern, and is a favourite resting-place with those who would study the language and customs of Germany. In fact, there is not much else to attract one, except a certain conventional society air, which seems to pervade all of its two score thousand inhabitants.

The architectural treasures of the city mostly bear eighteenth-century dates, from the great monumental gateway, by which one enters the city, and on which one reads, "*Regnante Carolo Frederico, M.B., S.R.I.P.E.,*" to the Academy of Fine Arts, really the most beautiful structure of the city, which dates only from 1845, though reproducing the Byzantine style of the early ages.

The great palace designed by Weinbrunner branches out like the leaves of a fan, and, if not the equal of Versailles or Fontainebleau, suggests them not a little in general effect.

The two chief churches of Carlsruhe are in no way great ecclesiastical edifices, or of any intrinsic artistic worth whatever. Both the principal Protestant place of worship and the Catholic edifice are from the designs of Weinbrunner, and are a confused mixture of pretty much all the well recognized details of style, with no convincing features of any. They are pretentious, gaudy, and quite out of keeping with religious feeling.

The Catholic edifice is a poor, ungainly imitation of the Pantheon at Rome, which reflects no dignity upon its author or the religion which it houses.

The Protestant church has its façade ornamented with six Corinthian columns—a weakly pseudo-classic style—which lead up to a tower which would be suitable enough to a country-side German parish church, but which, in a prosperous and gay little metropolis of pleasure, like Carlsruhe, is unappropriate and unfeeling, particularly when one recalls that it is a modern building which one contemplates. The window openings, too, recall rather those of a dwelling-house than of a religious edifice. So, when all is said and done, there is not much in favour of Carlsruhe's churches.

One link binds Carlsruhe with the traditions of ecclesiastical art in Germany, and that is a most acceptable statue of Ervin von Steinbach, the master-builder of Strasburg's cathedral. It flanks the principal portal of the Polytechnic School.

Darmstadt

Though more ancient than Carlsruhe, Darmstadt has a prosperous modern appearance, and consequently lacks those lovable qualities of a tumble-down mediæval town which usually surround architectural treasures of the first rank.

The Stadthaus, or Hôtel de Ville, dates from the fifteenth century, and the Palace from 1605 (in its reconstructed form); but there is nothing of sufficient interest about the churches to warrant the devotee of ecclesiastical architecture ever setting foot within their doors.

As delightful little cities, with tree-bordered promenades and a general air of prosperity and modernity, Carlsruhe and Darmstadt are well enough; but, as the setting for religious shrines, they are of no importance.

Behind the Stadthaus, in the old town, will be found the Protestant place of worship. It is in unconvincing Gothic, with nothing remarkable about its constructive elements, and little or nothing with respect to its details. One feature might perhaps arrest the attention. This is a retable of the conventional orthodox form which occupies the usual place—even in this Protestant church—at the end of the choir.

The Catholic church is situated on a great rectangular open place, known as the Wilhelminen Platz. It is a recent construction, and accordingly atrocious.

In form it is an enormous rotunda, one hundred and thirty-four feet in circumference, lighted by a shaft in the centre of its immense cupola. The porch by which one enters this rather pagan-looking structure is simple, and by far the most gracious feature of the edifice. On the frieze one reads, in great golden letters, the single word "Deo." In the lunette which surmounts this porch is a sculptured figure of the Virgin between two adoring angels, and on a marble tablet is engraved:

LUDOVICO
HASSIÆ ET AD RHENUM MAGNO DUCI
PATRI PATRIAE

The interior, more even than that of the church at Carlsruhe, is a weak imitation of the Pantheon at Rome.

The great dome is upheld by twenty-eight enormous Corinthian columns, but the walls are bare and without ornament of any sort.

The only accessory with any pretence at artistic expression is the altar. It is either remarkably fine, or else it looks so in comparison with its bare surroundings.

Wiesbaden

A conventional account of Wiesbaden would read something as follows:

"Wiesbaden, the capital of the Duchy of Nassau, is about an hour's drive by road from Mayence and three from Frankfort. It lies in a valley, encircled by low hills, behind which, on the north and northwest, rises the range of the Taunus Mountains, whose dark foliage forms an agreeable contrast to the brighter green of the meadows and the white buildings of the town. Within the last few years several new streets have been erected; the Wilhelmstrasse, fronting the promenades, would bear a comparison with some of the finest streets in Europe."

Such, in fact, is the description which usually opens the accounts one reads in the books of travel of a half or three-quarters of a century ago.

To-day Wiesbaden, as a "watering-place," doubtless retains all the virtues that it formerly possessed; but fashionable invalids have deserted Wiesbaden for Homburg.

All this is of course quite apart from the consideration of great churches; but great churches, for that matter, were quite apart from the considerations of most of the visitors to Wiesbaden.

The city possesses, however, a very satisfactory modern Catholic church, the work of the architect Hoffmann. It will not take rank with the mediæval masterpieces of many other places, but it demonstrates, as has only seldom been demonstrated, that it is possible to make a very satisfactory church building of to-day by copying pleasing details of other times.

Were it not that it is built in the red sandstone of the country, this fine edifice would be even more effective.

It is not a thoroughly consistent style that one sees. There is Byzantine, Romanesque, and avowedly Gothic details superimposed one upon another; but this is often seen in the masterpieces of other times, and, so long as the varieties are not put into quarrelling relationship with each other, it is perhaps allowable.

There is a triangular pediment above the grand portal which is certainly most singular, and may have been a product of the author's fancy alone. Nothing exactly similar is remembered elsewhere. In the main, however, the whole structure is reminiscent of much that, drawn from various sources, is the best of its kind.

The interior is divided into three naves by numerous great and small pillars of a polygonal form, the capitals only bearing any traces of modelling.

The high altar is decorated with some good sculptures, and there are a series of paintings, which might be modern, or might be ancient, so far as their unconvincing merits go.

Of the attraction of the waters and the pleasures of the society found at Wiesbaden during the season, nothing shall have place here, save to remark that the springs were famous even in the times of the Romans.

There is a "Greek chapel," built in 1855, at two kilometres from Wiesbaden. In the style of the sacred edifices of Moscow, this chapel was erected by the Emperor of Russia and by the Grand Duke Adolphe of Nassau to serve as the mausoleum of the Duchess Elizabeth of Nassau, a Russian princess.

GREEK CHAPEL, WIESBADEN

This fine memorial was also the work of the architect Hoffmann, and, though bizarre and unbeautiful enough from certain points of view, it is a highly successful transplanting of an exotic.

COAT OF ARMS, DARMSTADT

CHAPTER XIII
HEIDELBERG AND MANNHEIM

Heidelberg

As the ancient capital of the Lower Palatinate, Heidelberg early came into great prominence, though many of the details of its early history are lost in obscurity. The Romans have left traces of their passage, but the history of the early years of Christianity is but vaguely surmised.

Conrad of Hohenstaufen, brother of the red-bearded Frederick, came here, in 1148, as the first Count Palatine of the Rhine. The ruins of what is supposed to have been his once famous château are yet to be seen on the Geissberg.

In 1228 Heidelberg was declared the capital of the Palatinate under Otto of Wittelsbach, and became the residence of the Electors, who, for five hundred years, inhabited that other and more popularly famous château, which is known to all travellers on the Rhine as the "Castle of Heidelberg." In 1724, they chose Mannheim as their official residence.

Few cities of Europe have so frequently undergone such horrors of civilized warfare, if warfare ever *is* civilized, as has Heidelberg, though mostly it is associated in the popular mind of personally conducted tourists as a city of wine and beer drinking and general revelry and mirth.

The city has been five times bombarded, twice reduced to ashes, and three times taken by assault and pillaged.

To-day, it has recovered from all these disasters and takes its place as one of the most brilliant of the smaller commercial centres of the Rhine valley, though for that matter Heidelberg is situated some little distance from the river itself.

Of Heidelberg's population of perhaps twenty-five thousand souls, nearly one-third are Catholics, an exceedingly large proportion for a German town.

St. Peter's, the most ancient of Heidelberg's churches, contains many tombs of the Electors. In 1693 Mélac and his soldiers, after having thrown to the winds, at Speyer, the ashes of the emperors, rummaged about here in the church of St. Peter, and tore the bones of the nobles from their leaden caskets, throwing them broadcast in the streets. A Frenchman who remarked upon this sacrilege forgot that his own countrymen did the same at St. Denis's a hundred years later.

The principal church edifice of the city is St. Esprit's. Its architecture belongs to the fourteenth and fifteenth centuries, though it cannot be described as belonging to any precise style. Its interior is divided into two parts, which, curiously enough, were devoted to two distinct sects, the choir being consecrated to the Catholics and the nave being occupied by the Protestants. Jerome of Prague, a disciple of John Huss, harangued his believers in this church in times contemporary with that of Huss himself.

In the midst of the market-place is a statue of the Virgin, and facing the north side of the church is a house dating from 1492, known to-day by the sign of the Chevalier zum Ritter. Among the numerous ornaments of this fine mediæval dwelling-house is to be noted the following inscription:

> "*Si Jehova non edificet domum, frustra laborant œdificantes eam V.
> S. CXXVII.—Soli Deo gloria et perstat invicta Venus.*"

The University of Heidelberg, as presumably all readers of guide-books know, is the most ancient and the most celebrated in Germany. It was founded by Robert I. in 1386. Luther gave his dissertation here in 1515, hence, so far as its connection with religious matters goes, it is of great importance.

Its library was one of the most precious in Europe, but Tilly, who headed the Bavarians who entered Heidelberg in 1622, presented the greater part of it to Pope Leo XI. The valuable books and manuscripts remained in the Vatican, where they formed the Palatine Library, until the taking of Rome by the French in 1795. The rarest of the works were sent to Paris, whence they were returned to Heidelberg in 1815.

The theatrical-looking château of Heidelberg, which dominates the city and all the river valley round about, was built, in its most ancient parts, by the Elector Robert I., in the fourteenth century, though, for the most part, the walls that one gazes upon to-day are much more modern, having been erected by Frederick IV. in the sixteenth century.

In 1622 the castle was ravaged by the Spaniards, and, under the reign of Louis XIV. of France, it was bombarded by Turenne and by Mélac. Rebuilt with still greater magnificence, it was all but destroyed by lightning in 1764, since which time it has been practically abandoned and has become one of the most romantically picturesque ruins in Europe.

That portion of the edifice built by Otto Henry, who reigned 1556-59, is quite the most beautiful of all the various parts. It is known as the Hall of the Knights, and its plan and ornamentation is supposedly that of Michael Angelo.

The famous Heidelberg Tun is in one of the great vaulted chambers of the castle. The first of these utilitarian curiosities—Rhine wine matures best in large bodies—was built in 1535, and held 158,800 bottles. This tun was destroyed in the Thirty Years' War, and was replaced by a second which held 245,176 bottles, built by one Meyer, the cooper of the court. This tun was repaired in 1728 and exists to-day, but its grandeur is eclipsed by another made in 1751, during the electorate of Charles Theodore, which has a capacity of 284,000 bottles.

Mannheim

The modern-looking city of Mannheim has little ecclesiastical treasure to interest the student, although it is a wealthy and important centre.

HEIDELBERG AND ITS CASTLE

Its origin is very remote, and legend has it that it was the birthplace of a fabulous king of the Teutons called Mannus. Others have evolved its present nomenclature from a word taken from Norse mythology meaning the "dwelling-place of men." Either seems probable enough, and the reader must take his choice.

According to most authorities, the city first came into being in 765, but remained an insignificant hamlet up to the time of the Elector Frederick IV., who, in 1606, surrounded it with a city wall as a protection to the persecuted Protestants of the place. He also built the great château, the precursor of the present vast edifice, which contains, the guide-books say, fifteen hundred windows and five hundred rooms; as if that were its chief claim on one's attention.

The present structure was the former residence of the Electors of the Palatinate, and, though but a couple of hundred years old, is nevertheless an imposing and interesting edifice in more ways than one. To-day it is given over to collections of various sorts, Roman antiquities, old prints, and a gallery of paintings which contains some good work of Teniers and Wouvermans.

The Market and the Rathaus are the chief architectural attractions of this beautifully laid-out city, and its poor, mean little church of the Catholic religion is by no means an edifying expression of architectural art.

It is practically nothing more than what the French would call a *pavillon*, and is known as the *Unterpfaar*, the lower parish.

On the exterior wall one sees the pagan idea of caryatides carried out with Christian symbols, two figures of angels. There is also a mediocre statue representing "Faith," which it is difficult to accept as good art.

In the interior the short, narrow nave is separated from its aisles by four columns and two pillars on each side. The effect is somewhat that of a swimming bath. It is decidedly unchurchly.

There are a series of uninteresting tombs, and there is a high altar, gaudily rich with trappings, which would be a disgrace to a stage-carpenter.

There is little or no religious history connected with the city; but such devotional spirit as existed, and does exist to-day, ought to have left a better Christian memorial than that of the *Unterpfaar*.

CHAPTER XIV
WORMS

THIS most ancient city was the Vormatia of the Romans. It was devastated by Attila, and reëstablished by Clovis. At the beginning of the seventh century Brunhilda founded the bishopric, and Dagobert established his royal residence here in the years following. Afterward Charlemagne himself made it a resting-place many times, and held many Parliaments here.

In the tenth century Worms became a free city of the Empire, and in 1122 a Concordat was entered into between Pope Calixtus II. and the emperor, Henry V., concerning the ecclesiastical affairs of the city.

It was in the cathedral of Worms that the famous Diet of 1521 was held, when Charles V. declared Luther a heretic, and banished him from the Empire, for which indignity Luther is said to have remarked: "There are at Worms as many devils as there are tiles on the roof of its cathedral."

The city suffered much in the Thirty Years' War, and in 1689 was reduced to ashes by the armies of Louis XIV.

The cathedral of Worms was begun in 996 by Bishop Bouchard, and completed twenty years later by the Emperor Henry II. With its four fine towers and its two noble domes or cupolas, it ranks as one of the really great monuments of Christianity in Germany.

To-day, with its later additions, it is purely Romanesque, though built entirely after 1185, when Gothic was already making great strides elsewhere. Even here there is a decided ogival development to be noted in the vaulting of the nave.

Like the cathedrals at Mayence and Bonn, that at Worms offers the peculiarity of a double apside. The eastern termination is demi-round in the interior and square outside, while the westerly apse is polygonal both inside and out.

The cathedral was the only structure of note left standing in the city after the memorable siege of 1689.

The outline of this cathedral is most involved, with its high, narrow transepts, its two choirs crowned with cupolas and flanked with four lance-like towers. It is a suggestion, in a small way, of the more grandiose cathedral at Mayence, but it is by no means so picturesquely situated.

The portal of the façade shows some fine sculptures of the fourteenth century. One figure has given rise to much comment on the part of antiquaries and archeologists who have viewed it. It is a female figure mounted on a strange quadruped of most singular form, and like no manner of beast that ever walked the earth in the flesh.

It has been thought to be a symbolical allusion to the Queen Brunhilda, and again of the Church triumphant. It may be the former, but hardly the latter, at least such symbolism is not to be seen elsewhere.

The interior is of no special architectural value, if we except the contrast of the ogival vaulting with the Romanesque treatment otherwise to be observed.

There are numerous tombs and monuments, the chief being of three princesses of Burgundy who are buried here.

The church of St. Martin dates from the twelfth century, and Notre Dame from the thirteenth and fourteenth centuries. They are in every way quite as interesting as the cathedral, though their walls and vaults have been built up anew since the sacking of the city by the French in the seventeenth century.

The synagogue, recently restored, dates, as to its foundation, from the eleventh century, and is one of the most ancient in all Germany.

According to tradition, a Jewish colony was established at Worms 550 years B.C. This may or may not be well authenticated, — the writer does not know, — but no city in Germany in the middle ages had a colony of Jews more numerous, more venerated, or more ancient.

The Jews of Germany had three grand Rabbis, one at Prague, one at Frankfort, and the other at Worms. By the privilege of the Emperor Ferdinand, the Rabbi of Worms had precedence over the two others. They believed, according to a traditionary legend, that Worms was a part of the promised land, and it was said that the Jews' cemetery at Worms was made of soil brought from Jerusalem.

The wine-growers of Worms have given the name *Liebfraumilch* to the wine of the neighbourhood, particularly that which is gathered on the hillside gardens of the Church of Our Lady, and within the grounds of the ancient convent.

Near Worms is the ancient abbey of Lorsch, known in the middle ages as Lauresham and Lorse. The abbey was founded and dedicated (767-74) in the presence of Charlemagne, his wife Hildegarde, and his two sons, Charles and Pepin.

The churches of Trèves, of Metz, and of Cologne have, as we know, existed from very early times, and Maternus, an early Bishop of Cologne, is said to have been summoned to Rome in 313 to give his aid in deciding the Donatist controversy.

The oldest of all these Rhenish church foundations is thought to be that of Lorsch, whose bishop, Maximilian, died a martyr's death in the year 285.

The abbey became very wealthy, as was but natural under the patronage of such celebrated benefactors; but it fell a prey to the flames in 1090, and, in spite of immediate restoration, Lorsch never recovered its ancient splendour.

In 1232 it was incorporated with the archbishopric of Mayence, and the former imperial abbey became first, a priory of the monks of the order of Citeaux, and later of the Premonstentrationists.

The fine old twelfth-century church, rebuilt from that of 1100, has to-day become a grange, though only the ancient choir can be really said to exist.

The valuable library of Lorsch was fortunately saved at the Thirty Years' War, and, when the church was devastated by the Spaniards, was transported to Heidelberg.

The monastery at Lorsch is important as marking the transition between the Romanesque and Gothic in a manner not usually associated with the Rhine. One observes it notably in the porch, where the lower range of round-headed arcades is surmounted by a colonnade of sloping angular arches, which are certainly not Romanesque or classical, though, truth to tell, they resemble the clearly defined Gothic of France but little.

To-day the church of Lorsch presents no remarkable architectural features, and is simply an attractive and picturesquely environed building containing a few monuments worthy of note.

In olden times the town was protected by a strong château, constructed in 1348 by the Archbishop of Mayence, but no traces of it are left to-day.

CHAPTER XV

FRANKFORT

THERE is a legend which connects the foundation of Frankfort with a saying of Charlemagne's when he was warring against the Saxons.

Having fortunately escaped an attack from a superior force, by crossing the river Main during a thick fog, Charlemagne thrust his lance into the sand of the river-bank and exclaimed: "It is here that I will erect a city, in memory of this fortunate event, and it shall be known as '*Franken Furth,*'—'the Ford of the Franks.'"

The city owes its ancient celebrity, in part, to the crowning of the emperors, which, before Frankfort became an opulent commercial city, always took place here according to the laws promulgated in 1152 and 1356. Later the ceremony was transferred to Aix-la-Chapelle.

The first historical mention of the city was in 794, when Charlemagne convoked a Diet and a council of the Church.

Frankfort suffered greatly during the Thirty Years' War, in the War of Succession, and in the Revolution in 1793. Napoleon made the city a grand duchy in favour of the Prince-Primate Charles of Dalberg.

Of the ancient gateways of the city, but one remains to-day, that of Eschenheim, a fine monument of characteristically German features of the middle ages. It dates from the fourteenth century.

One of the principal attractions of Frankfort for strangers has ever been the Juden Gasse,—the street of the Jews. It dates from 1662. As one enters, on the left, at No. 148, is the *maison paternelle* of the celebrated Rothschilds.

The cathedral at Frankfort is consecrated to St. Bartholomew. It was begun under the Carlovingians and was only completed in the fourteenth century.

At the extreme western end is a colossal tower which ranks as one of the latest and most notable pure Gothic works in Germany (1415-1509). Its architect was John of Ettingen, and it rises to a height of one hundred and sixty-three feet.

The façade of the cathedral is entirely lacking in a decorative sense, and the lateral portal, on the south, is much encumbered by surrounding structures, though one sees peeping out here and there evidences of a series of finely sculptured figures.

Above the entrance to the cloister is an equestrian statue of St. Bartholomew, a masterwork of sixteenth-century German sculpture. The skull of the apostle is preserved in the church proper.

FRANKFORT CATHEDRAL

The general plan of the church is that of a Greek cross, but the termination which holds the choir is of much narrower dimensions than the other three arms.

The grand nave offers nothing of remark, but the side aisle to the right contains a fine "Ecce Homo" in bas-relief, placed upon the tomb of the Consul Hirde, who died in 1518. Unfortunately the heads of many of the figures, including that of the Christ, are badly scarred and broken.

In the right transept are a series of very ancient German paintings and a number of escutcheons, coloured and in high relief, commemorating benefactors of the church.

The walls in the choir are covered with ancient frescoes of the frankly German school. They undoubtedly date back to the fifteenth century, at least.

At the right of the choir is the tomb of the Emperor Gunther of Schwarzburg, who died here in 1349.

Above the high altar is a fine tabernacle,—a feature frequently seen in German churches,—of silver-gilt. To the left is an ancient iron grille of remarkable workmanship.

At the head of the left aisle of the nave is a chapel containing a "Virgin at the Tomb," a coloured sculpture of the fifteenth century, surmounted by a very ornate Gothic *baldaquin*.

In the left transept is the tomb of a knight of Sachsenhausen bearing the date of 1371. Here, too, is a somewhat dismantled and fragmentary astronomical clock of the species best seen at Strasburg.

The Protestant church of St. Nicholas is a fine ogival edifice, which in more recent times was profaned by commercial uses. It has since been restored and its red sandstone fabric is surmounted by a fine spire.

The interior shows a remarkably fine ogival choir as its chief feature, an organ-buffet carried out in the same style, which is most unusual, and a charming wooden staircase with an iron railing leading to a tribune at the crossing. All of the accessories are modern, but the effect is unquestionably good.

The church of St. Leonard dates from the thirteenth century and possesses as its chief exterior features two rather diminutive spires. The Emperor Frederick II. ceded the site to the city, for the erection of a church, at the above mentioned period.

The church of St. Catherine is of the seventeenth century, and, like most religious erections of its age, is in no way remarkable. The exterior, however, shows a rather pleasing square tower, which is surmounted by an octagonal campanile. The interior has some fine modern paintings, well painted and equally well displayed.

The church of St. Paul was formerly a Carmelite foundation. It is strictly modern, and was only completed in 1833. Its form is rather more pagan than Christian, being simply a great oval, one hundred and thirty odd feet in length by one hundred and eight in width. The interior is surrounded by a fine Ionic colonnade.

In 1848 St. Paul's was appropriated to the sessions of the German parliament, to which purpose the structure was well suited.

The Liebfrauenkirche has a fine "Adoration" sculptured above its principal portal. It is a good example of German sculpture in stone. Within the walls is a painting attributed to Martin Schoen which merits consideration.

COAT OF ARMS, FRANKFORT

CHAPTER XVI

MAYENCE

Mayence has been variously called the city of Gutenberg, and of the Minne-singers. The Romans in Augustus's time had already fortified it and given it the name of Magontiacum.

Near Mayence is the cenotaph of Drusus, where his ashes were interred after the funeral oration by Augustus, who came expressly from Rome into Gaul for the purpose.

Mayence as a Roman colony was a military post of great importance, and the key to the fertile provinces watered by the Rhine.

An episcopal seat was established here in the third century, but Christianity had a hard struggle against wars and internal disorders of many kinds.

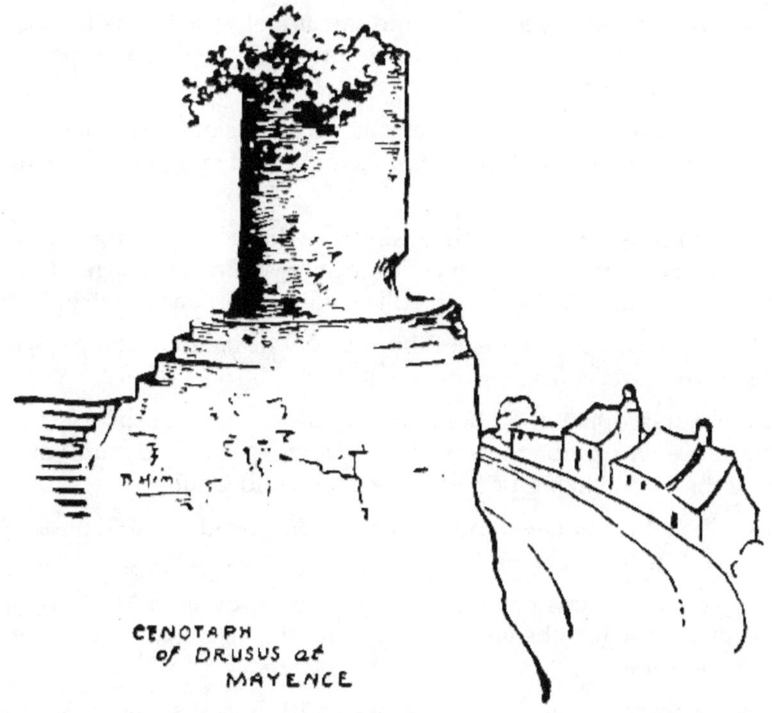

CENOTAPH OF DRUSUS, MAYENCE

Many times the city has been devastated and rebuilt. In 718 Bishop Sigibert surrounded the city by a series of walls, and between 975 and 1011 Archbishop Willigis built the cathedral and the church of St. Stephen, at which time the real Christianizing of Mayence may be said to have begun.

The venerable old cathedral has many times been battered and bruised, and fire and bombardment have reduced its original form into somewhat of a hybrid thing, but it remains to-day the most stupendously imposing and bizarre cathedral of all the Rhine valley.

In general its architecture is decidedly not good, but it is interesting, and therein lies the chief charm of a great church.

During the siege of the French the cathedral at Mayence, in 1793, again took fire, and the western end of the roof of the choir, the nave, and the transept all succumbed.

For ten years it remained in this state, until the order for restoration came from the omnific Bonaparte, then first consul. In 1804 the edifice was consecrated anew.

In the year 636 there was held at Mayence an assembly of the bishops of the Frankish kingdom convoked by Dagobert, then king.

Among the bishops of Mayence none had a reputation so popular as that of St. Boniface, who had been sent out by Pope Gregory III. as a missioner to the Rhine country.

Boniface had given Pepin-le-Bref the sacrament at Soissons in 752, upon the fall of the Merovingian dynasty, and in return King Pepin gave the bishopric of Mayence to St. Boniface.

In 813 a numerous council met here, at the orders of Charlemagne, under the presidency of Hildebold, Archbishop of Cologne and chaplain of the holy palace at Rome.

In the tenth century the church at Mayence did not fall to the sad state that it did elsewhere. Ecclesiastical writers of France have always referred to this period as *le siècle de plomb*, but at Mayence it still steadily approached the golden age.

Mayence was still distinguished by the zeal of its archbishops, whose good influences were far-reaching.

Under the episcopate of St. Boniface and his immediate successors the cathedral of Mayence was probably a wooden structure, as were many of the earlier churches of the evangelizing period in Germany and Gaul.

The work on the mediæval cathedral was completed by 1037, under Archbishop Bardon, and its consecration took place in presence of the Emperor Conrad II.

Twelve years after this ceremony, Pope Leo IX. came to Mayence and held a famous council, at which the emperor was present, accompanied by the principal nobles of the empire.

The cathedral fell a prey to the flames in 1087, as well as three other neighbouring churches, say the older chronicles, and the ancient structure disappeared almost entirely, so far as its original outline was concerned.

Archbishop Conrad of Wittelsbach restored the nave inside of three years, and the monument again took on some of its ancient magnificence. In 1198 Emperor Philip of Suabia, son of Frederick Barbarossa, was solemnly crowned in this cathedral by the Archbishop of Tarentaise, the Archbishop of Mayence being at that time in the Holy Land.

The twelfth-century work doubtless was erected on the foundations of Archbishop Bardon's structure.

The restoration of the transept and the western choir followed, and the work went on more or less intermittently until the middle of the thirteenth century, when the fabric approached somewhat the appearance that it has to-day.

The completed structure was consecrated in 1239, and, save the chapels of the late thirteenth and fourteenth centuries, the body of the edifice has not greatly changed since that time.

During the Thirty Years' War it became practically a ruin, however, though its later rebuilding was on the original lines.

In 1793 the revolution which sprang up in France forced its way to the Rhine, and, when Mayence was besieged, the roof of the cathedral caught fire and the church itself was pillaged and profaned.

For a long time the old cathedral remained abandoned, as after an invasion of barbarians, which is about what the revolutionists proved themselves to be. In 1803 Napoleon saw fit to order it to be restored, and in the following year it was returned to its adherents.

The ancient metropolis, however, lost the distinction which had been given to it in Roman times, and the glory first brought upon it by St. Boniface lapsed when the arch-episcopal see was suppressed. Mayence is now merely a bishopric, a suffragan of Cologne.

In its general plan the cathedral at Mayence follows the outlines of a Latin cross, though its length is scarcely more than double its width.

It is most singular in outline and has two choirs, one at either end, as is a frequent German custom, and the sky-line is curiously broken by the six towers which pierce the air, no two at the same elevation.

There are three portals which give entrance from various directions. There is yet a fourth entrance from the market-place, which takes one through a sort of cellar which is not in the least churchly and is decidedly unpleasant.

The principal nave is supported by nine squared pillars, which are hardly beautiful in themselves, but which are doubtless necessary because of the great weight they have to bear.

In the Gothic choir is a heavy *baldaquin* in marble, bearing figures of the twelve apostles. The high altar is directly beneath the cupola, or lantern, of the principal tower. It is quite isolated, and has neither flanking columns nor a *baldaquin*. On feast-days it is brilliantly set forth with candelabra in a fashion which would be theatrical, if it were not churchly.

MAYENCE CATHEDRAL

Behind this altar is the space reserved for the clergy, a somewhat unusual arrangement, but not a unique one. At the extreme end is the bishop's throne.

The general appearance of the interior constructive elements would seem to place the work as a whole well within the thirteenth century, though the extreme easterly portion is more ancient still.

There is very little of pure Gothic to be noted. Mostly the fabric is a reproduction of the Lombard style, though much undeniably Gothic ornament is used. The bays of the nave are singularly narrow and of great height, almost the reverse of the pure Italian manner of building which elsewhere made itself strongly felt along the Rhine. The height of these bays is more than two and a half times the width. The bays of German churches, in general, have a much greater length than those of Italy, and herein is a marked difference between the Italian and German styles in spite of other resemblances.

There are in the cathedral numerous paintings of questionable artistic worth and an abundance of coloured glass, which is condemned as comparatively modern and of no especial interest.

The altar of St. Martin, with statues of Sts. Martin and Boniface, is near the baptistery. There are eight lateral chapels, out of fifteen in all, which are bare and without altars, showing a poverty—whatever may have been the cause—which is deplorable.

In the Bassenheim chapel is a remarkable marble group taken from the church of Notre Dame, a Gothic edifice destroyed during the siege of 1793.

There are numerous and beautiful funeral monuments scattered about the church, the most celebrated being that which surmounts the tomb of Frastrada, the third wife of Charlemagne, who died in 794, and was originally interred in the church of St. Alban. The remains were removed to the cathedral when the former church was burned in 1552.

On the tomb of Frastrada one may read the following eighth-century inscription:

> *"Frastradana, pia Caroli conjux vocitata,*
> *Christo dilecta, jacet hoc sub marmore tecta,*
> *Anno septingentesimo nonagesimo quarto,*
> *Quem numerum metro claudere musa negat*
> *Rex pie, quem gessit Virgo, licet hic cinerescit,*
> *Spiritus hœres sit patriæ quæ tristia nescit."*

There are also the tombs of thirty-two archbishops,—a veritable valhalla of churchly fame. Mostly these tombs are ordinary enough, those of Archbishop Berthould of Hennéberg and of the doyen of the chapter being alone remarkable.

The chapel of St. Gothard, a dependency of the cathedral, was built by Archbishop Adelbert I. in 1135-36.

The ancient cloister at Mayence dates from the mid-thirteenth century. Archbishop Siegfried was responsible for the work which was consecrated in the year

1243 in the presence of the Emperor Conrad, on the occasion of a synod which was being held at Mayence at that time. The cloister, as it exists to-day, is made up in part of this ancient work and in part of a more modern construction, this latter being the portion which adjoins the church proper.

The chapter-house was built at the end of the twelfth century or at the beginning of the thirteenth. It is a square apartment covered with an ogival vaulting which springs from a range of pillars with delicately sculptured foliaged capitals. It is decidedly the architectural gem of this composite edifice.

To the north of the cathedral, in the Speise-Markt, is a remarkably fine fountain, restored, or perhaps rebuilt, in the sixteenth century by the Archbishop of Mayence. A *baldaquin* supported by three pillars rises above a well or spring, and on a stone slab one reads the following inscription in letters of gold:

> *"Divo Karolo V Cesare semp Augus. post victoria gallicam rege ipso ad Ticinum superato ac capto triumphante, fatalique rusticorū per Germnia (sic) cospiratione prostratâ, Alber. card. et archiep. Mog. fontē hanc vetustate dilapsa ad civiū suorum posteritatisque usum restitui curavit anno MDXXVI."*

The Meistersingers of Mayence owed their origin to Henry Misnie, who, according to some authorities, was a canon of the Church, and, according to others, a doctor of theology. He was devoted, at any rate, to poetry, and was, in the fourteenth century, founder of the school of the Master-singers.

He dedicated a great part of his songs to the Virgin, his ideal of all that was pious and good. Later he widened the range of his dedications to include all of the female sex, and beautiful women in particular. He is known in the history of German poetry under the name of Henry von Frauenlob.

His death caused a universal sorrow among the fair sex of Mayence, who gave his funeral such honours as were never before known.

The majority of the great procession which conducted his remains to the tomb, which had been prepared in the cathedral, were women, "eight of the most beautiful bearing a crown of roses, lilies, and myrtle." This is a pretty enough sentiment, but it seems quite inexplicable to-day. History records that the master-singer's favourite drink was the noble wine of the Rhingau, and it is commonly supposed to have inspired many of his beautiful songs.

Legend steps in and says that "the naves of the cathedral were inundated by the libations which went on at this funeral ceremony."

A modern white marble monument, put into place in 1842, and replacing one that had previously disappeared, stands as a memorial to the sweet singer of the praises of women.

CHAPTER XVII

BACHARACH, BINGEN, AND RUDESHEIM

Bacharach

BACHARACH is famous for its legends and its wine. With the former is associated the ruins of St. Werner's Church, a fragment of exquisite flamboyant Gothic, though built of what looks like a red sandstone. The Swedes demolished it in the Thirty Years' War, but the lantern and the eastern lancet window still remain to suggest its former great beauty.

This beautiful chapel was built as a memorial to the child Werner, whose body was fabled to have been thrown by the Jews, his supposed murderers, into the Rhine at Oberwesel. Instead of floating down-stream with the current, it went up-stream as far as Bacharach, where it was recovered.

There is at Bacharach a twelfth-century church in the Byzantine style, which is now a Protestant temple. It is an incongruous affair in spite of the fact that the style is fairly pure of its kind, so far as the body of the church is concerned. Surmounting it is a needle-like spire which rises above the crenelated battlement of its tower in a most fantastic manner.

The city walls have great ornamental and picturesque qualities, and were, in former days, defended by twelve towers of imposing strength.

The evolution of the name of Bacharach is decidedly non-Christian. It is frankly pagan, being descended from *Bacchi ara*,—the altar of Bacchus,—which was the name originally given to a rock in the midst of the river, which, in varying seasons, is sometimes covered by the flood, and again quite dry. When its surface appears to the light of day, the vineyard owner hails it as a sign of good vintage.

In proof of the quality of the wines of Bacharach, it is said that Pope Pius II. used every year to have a great tun of it brought to Rome for his special use, and that the Emperor Wenceslas granted their freedom to the citizens of Nuremberg in return for four tuns of the wine of Bacharach. To-day Bacharach is, with Cologne, the great wine centre of the Rhine valley.

Asmanhausen, a few miles up the river, is the central mart for the red wines of the Rhine. Near Asmanhausen is Ehrenfels, where the Archbishops of Mayence had a château in the thirteenth century. The château is still there, but it is nothing more than a magnificent ruin.

BACHARACH

BISHOP HATTO'S MOUSE TOWER

Bingen

Opposite Ehrenfels is Bingen, with its Mäuseturm. The chief sentimental memory of Bingen is unquestionably the legend of Bishop Hatto and his "Mouse Tower on the Rhine."

The legend of Hatto, versified by Southey, has stamped the memory of the Mouse Tower and its associations so indelibly upon the mind that it overshadows in interest all else in the vicinity.

> " 'Tis the safest place in Germany;
> The walls are high, and the shores are steep,
> And the stream is strong and the water deep."

How the rats came and —

> ". . . whetted their teeth against the stones
> And how they picked the Bishop's bones" —

is an old story with which children have been regaled for generations past.

The great white "Mouse Tower" stands to-day on its tiny island in the middle of the waters of the Rhine, between Bingen and Ehrenfels, to perpetuate the story, while its ruined walls look down, as they always have, on the steady flow of the Rhine water, making its way from the place of its birth in the Canton of Grisons to the cold waters of the German ocean off the coast of Holland.

Rudesheim

Rudesheim, but a small town of less than three thousand inhabitants, is noted for its wines and its ruins. Its church, though a fifteenth-century edifice of more than ordinary beauty, — if we except its nondescript spire, — comes decidedly last in the city's list of attractions.

The remains of the four châteaux in the neighbourhood are the chief object of the casual tourist.

The town is the centre of a vineyard, the grapes being grown in great profusion near it. The favourable nature of the locality for grape-growing was discovered, it is said, by Charlemagne, who, remarking the rapid disappearance of the snow on the slopes about Rudesheim, declared his belief that fine wine might be grown there. Sending to France for some plants, they were placed in the earth, and have ever since yielded a grape worthy of their parentage, a grape still called Orleans.

From this town the tourist may make a pleasant excursion to the Nieder-wald, — having first given his attention to the history of Rudesheim, once the seat of an imperial court held in the Nieder Burg, — and scan its four ancient castles. Of these, one belonged for a time to Prince Metternich, who, however, sold it to Count Ingelheim, its present possessor; another is picturesquely posted at the up-per part of the town, and still retains some curious relics of the Bromser family, its old possessors. A tradition still exists, telling how Hans Bromser, being taken captive in Jerusalem, made a vow to Heaven that if released he would dedicate his only daughter to the service of the Church. Gaining his liberty soon afterward, he returned to the Rhine to find the child he had left when he started for the Crusades grown to womanhood; and he learned also that, secure of her father's sanction, she had betrothed herself to a youthful knight. Love and duty well-nigh rent the maiden's heart in twain, till love conquered, and she begged her stern parent to relent. This he refused to do, and threatened her with a father's curse should she marry.

Despairing, she threw herself into the Rhine, and her body floated downstream as far as Bishop Hatto's Mouse Tower, at Bingen. This gave rise to another legend, that when the surface of the waters is troubled it is caused by the uneasy spirit of Bromser's daughter, wrestling with the dreadful fate to which she was driven.

COAT OF ARMS, BINGEN

CHAPTER XVIII
LIMBURG

The cathedral of Limburg-on-Lahn, not farther from the juncture of the Lahn and Rhine than is Frankfort-on-the-Main, may well be considered a Rhine cathedral.

The Lahn is by no means so powerful a stream as is the Main or the Neckar; nor is it either picturesque, or even important as a waterway.

It has this one virtue, however: it forms a setting to Limburg's many-spired cathedral that is truly grand.

Limburg played a great part in the middle ages, and its origin goes far back into antiquity. Under Drusus a *castellum* was erected here, which was destroyed by the Franks and the Alemanni.

The counts of the lower Lahn province were among the most powerful in all Germany. They gave their city the name of Roemercastel, which name, to some extent, may be said to live up to to-day. Later the Franks called it Lintburc, from the little river Linther, which flows into the Lahn at this point.

The cathedral of Limburg is the most imposing and homogeneous of all the *romano-ogival* edifices of Germany.

Consecrated to St. George, this church dates from the latter years of the twelfth century and the early part of the thirteenth. It was erected by Count Henry of Nassau, and replaced two more ancient edifices on the same site.

Without a doubt it is a mediæval monument which stands supreme in its class, though its grandeur comes not so much from mere magnitude as it does from the general disposition of its plan, and the wonderful blending of the transition elements which, after all is said and done, in Germany, are not elsewhere very pronounced.

The seven spires and towers of this cathedral form a wonderful grouping and make a sky-line more broken than that of any other great church in all Europe.

There is a certain symmetry about this outline, but it is not pyramidal, after the manner of the cathedral at Bonn. In short, it is reminiscent only of itself.

On the west are a pair of massive towers with conical caps, which give a façade at once remarkable and distinguished.

Flanking the north transept are two smaller towers, and the same arrangement is found just opposite on the south.

LIMBURG CATHEDRAL

Above rises the great central octagon, surmounted in turn by a dwindling octagonal spire, not beautiful in itself with its steeply inclined slate or lead roofing, but which, under all atmospheric conditions, lends a harmony to and is a key-note of the whole structure which is wonderfully effective.

The interior plan is conventional and simple enough, consisting of the usual three naves, with an easterly apse, surrounded by an ambulatory and flanking chapel.

Within, as well as from the outside, the effect is one of an ampleness which is not borne out by the actual dimensions, which fact, of course, shows most able design and execution.

The elevation of the nave, choir, and transepts is divided into four ranges of openings, such as are seen at Soissons in the Isle of France, and, in a less complete form, in Notre Dame at Paris.

This has always been a daring procedure, but in this case it has been carried out with success, and gives the desired effect,—that of ampleness and height.

In the clerestory windows are found the rounded arches which mark the link which binds the Gothic arches elsewhere in the fabric with the earlier Romanesque style.

The vaulting is of the Gothic order throughout, with gracefully proportioned shafts and full-flowered capitals.

All this preserves the simple elements of early Gothic in so impressive a way that the observer will quite overlook, or at least make allowance for, the row of round-headed windows aloft.

The triforium gallery is a charming feature, and has seldom been found so highly developed outside of an early Gothic church. In general the feature is French, and this is perhaps the only example outside France which is so reminiscent of that variety frequently to be met with in the cathedrals of the Isle of France.

The triforium is pierced through to the nave by a series of double narrow arches enclosed within a larger broad-framed arch, while in the transepts and choir the desired effect is accomplished by tripled arches with the same general scheme of arrangement.

With regard to furnishings and accessories, this great cathedral is singularly complete.

There is a highly ornate pulpit in sculptured wood which some will consider the peer of any seen elsewhere. It is decorated further by a series of painted wooden statues of the saints, Nicholas, Ambrose, Augustin, Gregory, and Jerome.

There is a fine *custode* covering a pyx, which is surmounted by a fifteenth-century *baldaquin*, and a tomb of a former canon, ornamented in bas-relief.

There is also a pair of baptismal fonts, enormous in size and said to be contemporaneous with the foundation of the cathedral.

A tomb of Daniel of Mutersbach, a knight who died in 1475, is placed in one of the chapels at the crossing, and near by is a mausoleum to that Conrad who, by virtue of a charter given by Louis in 909, founded the church which preceded the present edifice on this site.

It bears the following inscription in the barbarous Latin of the time:

CLAUDITUR HOC TUMULO PER QUEM
NUNC SERVITUS ISTO
FIT CELEBRIS TEMPLO, LAUS, VIRTUS,
GLORIA CHRISTO.

CHAPTER XIX

COBLENZ AND BOPPART

Coblenz

It is an open question as to whether the charming little city of Coblenz is more delightful because of itself, or because of its proximity to the famous fortress of Ehrenbreitstein, —"the broad stone of honour."

> "Here Ehrenbreitstein with her shatter'd wall
> Black with the miner's blast upon her height,
> Yet shows of what she was, when shell and ball
> Rebounding idly on her strength did light."

The city occupies a most romantically and historically endowed situation at the junction of the Moselle and the Rhine.

At Coblenz the sons of Charlemagne met to divide their father's empire into France, Germany, and Italy; there also Edward III. in 1338 met the Emperor Louis, and was by him appointed vicar of the empire; and at Coblenz the French raised a monument to commemorate the subjugation of Russia. Soon after the inscription was finished, the Russian commander entered Coblenz in pursuit of Napoleon. With memorable and caustic wit he left the inscription as it stood, just adding, "Vu et approuvé par nous, Commandant Russe de la Ville de Coblence, Janvier 1er, 1814." Here also is the monument to the young and gallant General Marceau, killed at the battle of Altenkirchen, 1796.

> "By Coblenz, on a rise of gentle ground,
> There is a small and simple pyramid,
> Crowning the summit of the verdant mound:
> Beneath its base are hero's ashes hid."

The Moselle, which joins the Rhine at Coblenz, was, like the Rhine itself, referred to by Cæsar.

The pleasant valley of the Moselle—indeed it is one of the *pleasantest* (which is a vague term, but one easily understood by all) in all Europe—was celebrated by one of the longer poems of Ausonius, who wrote in the fourth century.

For those who would translate the original, his description will not be found inapropos to-day:

> *"Qua sublimis apex longo super ardua tractu*
> *Et rupes et aprica jugi, flexusque sinusque*

Vitibus adsurgunt naturalique theatro."

Vines then, as now, clothed the slopes of the hills and cliffs which sheltered the deep-cut stream.

A Roman governor of Gaul once proposed to unite the Moselle with the Saône (as it is to-day, by means of the Canal de l'Est), and thus effect a waterway across Europe from the North Sea to the Mediterranean.

The church of St. Castor stands on the spot of the famous conference between the sons of Charlemagne. It is one of the most ancient of the Rhine churches, and was founded by Louis the Pious in 836.

Of this early church but little remains to-day except some distinct features to be noted in the choir.

The four towers form a remarkable outline, and two of them, at least as to their lower ranges, are undoubtedly of the eleventh century.

In this church are a series of remarkable decorations, one on the wall above the spring of the nave arches, another above the entrance of the choir aisle, and yet another in the semicircular roofing of the apse. It may be a question as to how far such decorations are in really good taste, but they certainly lend a warmth and brilliancy to an edifice that might otherwise be cold and unfeeling.

Many are the historic incidents connected with this venerable building. The notification of the sons of Louis the Pious took place in 870; the reconciliation of Henri IV. of Germany with his sons occurred in 1105; St. Bernard preached the Crusades here before a vast congregation, recruiting for the army for the East over one thousand citizens of Coblenz alone.

Near the church of St. Castor is the house of the Teutonic Order, of fine Gothic design, but to-day turned into a military magazine.

On a hill overlooking the city was the famous Chartreuse convent, the ruins of which are now swallowed up by Forts Constantine and Alexander.

The bridge which crosses the Moselle at this point is in itself a wonderful old relic. It spans the river on fourteen arches, and dates from 1344, save that its watch-tower was built at a later day.

The bridge of boats which crosses the Rhine, on thirty-six pontoons, partakes of the same characteristics as its brother at Mayence, though by no means is it so celebrated.

Above Coblenz the Rhine narrows considerably, and the mountains and hill-tops draw in until one's progress, by water, is almost as if it were through a cañon.

Niederlahnstein has a fine ruined church in St. John's, whence it is but a short distance to Boppart.

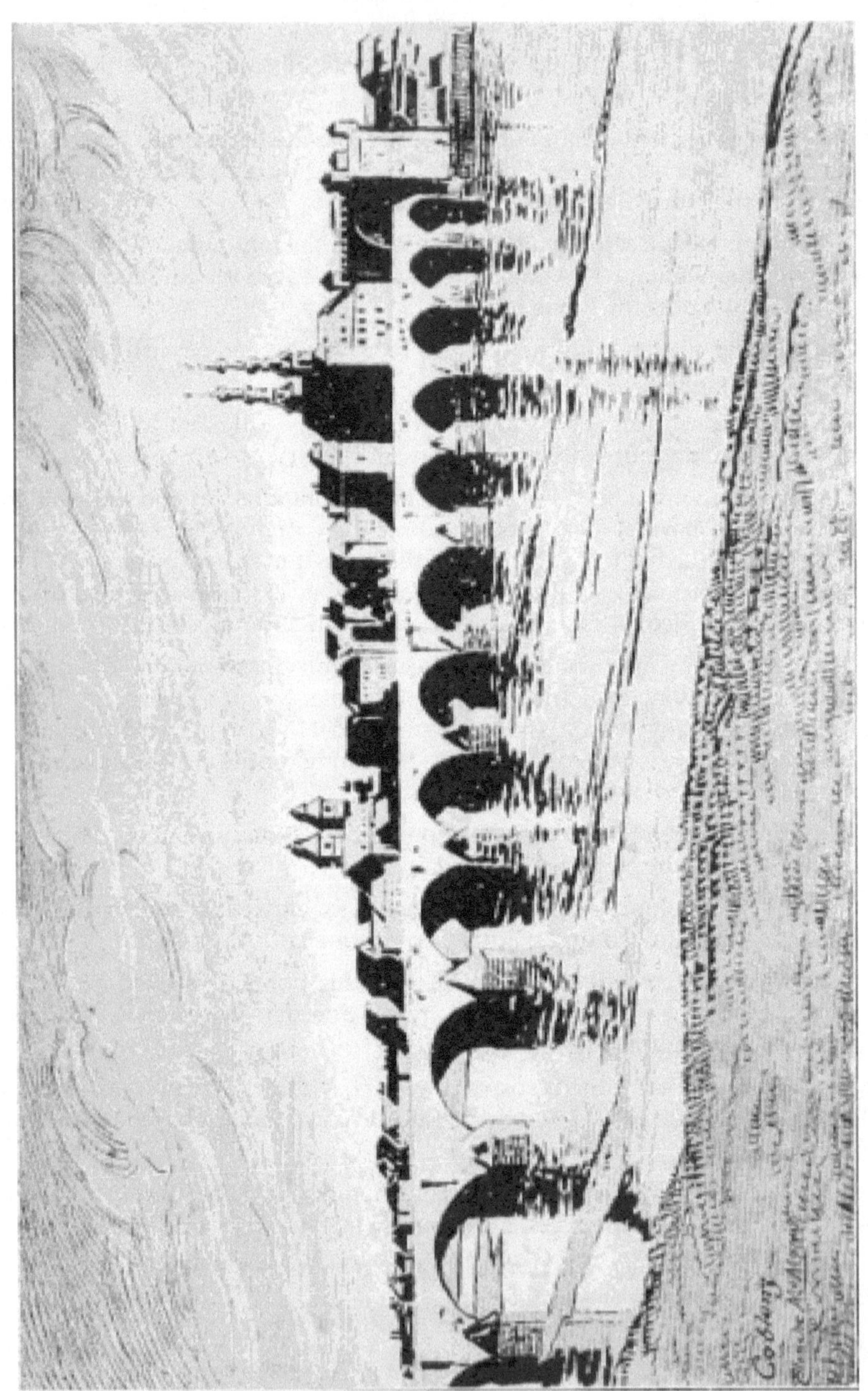

COBLENZ AND ITS BRIDGE

GENERAL VIEW OF BOPPART

Boppart

Boppart was the ancient *Bandobriga* of the Romans, and, like many another place along the Rhine, is closely linked with the memory of Drusus.

Boppart was made an imperial city, and many Diets were held within its walls.

The Hauptkirche, with its twin-jointed spires, was built about the year 1200.

It is thoroughly Romanesque, if we except the spires which are linked together by a sort of galleried vestibule, after a manner that is neither Romanesque nor anything else.

The inside galleries over the aisles (*männerchöre*) are interesting, though by no means a unique feature in Rhine churches.

There is a queer intermixture of pointed and round-headed arches in both the nave and choir, but nothing to indicate that it was anything but a Romanesque influence that inspired the builders of this not very appealing church.

The vestibule which joins the spires, and the most unusual groining of the vaulting of the body of the church, are two features which the expert will linger over and marvel at, but they have not much interest for the lay observer who will prefer to stroll along the river-bank and pick out charming vistas for his camera.

The convent of Marienburg, which rises high on the hillside back of the town, has an ancient history and was a vast foundation to which references are continually met with in history. To-day it is a hydropathic establishment for semi-invalids and devotees of bridge and tea parties.

The Carmelite church contains some richly carved sixteenth-century monuments, now somewhat mutilated, but very beautiful.

The *Templehof* perpetuates the fact that it was the Knights Templars of Boppart who first mounted the breach at the storming of Ptolemais in the third crusade.

This completes the list of Boppart's ecclesiastical monuments.

In the fourteenth century the town was a "free imperial city"; but, following upon political dissension with its neighbours, it was returned to the guardianship of the Archbishop of Trèves.

Previously it would appear that the inhabitants had not been very religious, but the archbishop was able to induce them to build him a château here as a place of temporary residence; "the first service," says the chronicle of the time, "which we have rendered our gracious master."

COAT OF ARMS, COBLENZ

CHAPTER XX
LAACH AND STOLZENFELS

Laach

Back of Coblenz is the charming little lake of Laach, at the other end of which is the picturesque but deserted abbey of Laach, one of the most celebrated, architecturally and historically, of all the religious edifices along the Rhine.

Once a Benedictine convent, it was pillaged and its inmates dispersed during the overflow of the French Revolution, and is now naught but a ruin, though in many respects a grandly preserved one.

ABBEY OF LAACH (RESTORED)

The abbey was founded in 1093 by Henry II. of Laach, Count Palatine of Lower Lorraine, and the first Count Palatine of the Rhine.

Its magnificent church, built in the most acceptable Gothic, contains the remains of its founder and many nobles.

The monks of the abbey were, in the middle ages, greatly celebrated for their knowledge of the sciences and their hospitality. Their library was richly stored with bibliographical treasures, and they possessed a fine collection of paintings. To-day the abbey and its dependencies is but a shadow of its former self; its library and its picture-gallery have disappeared, and, early in the nineteenth century, the establishment was sold for a price so small that it would be a sacrilege to mention it.

STOLZENFELS CASTLE

Stolzenfels

The mention of the castle of Stolzenfels hardly suggests anything churchly or devout, though those who know the history of this most picturesque of all Rhine castles (restored though it be) know also that it was an early foundation of Archbishop Arnold of Trèves in the thirteenth century, and was, during the century following, the residence of his successors.

Placed high upon its *"proud rock,"* the restored fabric to-day wonderfully resembles the castled-crag of one's imagination.

Archbishop Werner of Strasburg also made it his residence in turn, and later the English princess betrothed to the Emperor Frederick II. of the Hohenstaufen dynasty was entertained there.

The castle was nearly destroyed by the French in 1688, and in 1825 the ruin was made over to the then prince royal, afterward King of Prussia.

Within the reconstructed walls, topped with a series of crenelated battlements, after the true mediæval manner, one finds an ample courtyard, from which lead the entrances to the various parts of the vast fortress.

Innumerable apartments open out one from the other, all forming a great museum filled with all manner of curios and relics.

In a corner of one great room was long kept (they may or may not be there yet; the writer does not know) the Austrian and Swiss standards taken in the Thirty Years' War.

There was also a cabinet containing the sabre of Murat, taken at Waterloo; the sabres of Blucher, of Poniatowski, and Sobieski; and the swords of the Duc d'Albe and De Tilly; and, incongruously enough, a knife and fork said to have belonged to Andreas Hofer, the hero of the Tyrol.

In the chamber of the king is a magnificent piece of ecclesiastical furniture in the form of a processional cross said to date from the eighth century.

The fine Gothic chapel is decidedly the gem of the whole fabric and its accessories, and, though only finished in its completeness, during the present day, it is a master copy of the best style of the Gothic era.

COAT OF ARMS, LAACH

CHAPTER XXI
ANDERNACH AND SINZIG

Andernach

ANDERNACH is one of the oldest cities in the Rhine valley, and grew up out of one of Drusus's camps, which was built here when the town was known as *Antonacum*.

This was its early history, as given by Ammien Marcellin; and a later authority mentions it as the second city of the electorate of Trèves (*Die Andre Darnach*).

In the records of Drusus's time, there is a reference to a château here, which was the fiftieth he had built upon the banks of the Rhine.

The kings of Austrasia had their palace here as well, so the place became a political and strategic city of very nearly the first rank.

In the middle ages Andernach shone brilliantly among the centres of commerce in the Rhine valley.

Charles V. was responsible for a battle between the inhabitants of Linz and those of Rhieneck and Andernach, in which nearly all the latter were massacred.

To soften any hard feeling that might still exist, a sermon was always preached, up to the last century, in the market-place, on St. Bartholomew's Day, urging the people to forgive their enemies. The records tell, however, that on one occasion an unfortunate inhabitant of Linz was discovered in Andernach, and that he was forthwith put to death in most unchristianlike fashion.

The Gate of Coblenz at Andernach is generally regarded as an ancient Roman work, though not of the monumental order usual in works of its kind.

The present fortifications date from the fifteenth century, as does the picturesque watch-tower by the waterside.

With Andernach is identified the tradition of a Count Palatine, who, returning from the Holy Wars, was persuaded by a false friend that his lady had proved faithless; and, without listening to excuse, drove her forth to the woods. In the forest she found shelter with her youthful son, lodging in caves and living on fruits and herbs for many years. One day her husband, having lost his companions in the chase, came by accident upon her place of concealment. The wife of his bosom, carefully nurtured in her youth, but now living unattended in the wilds, and his son, now grown into a fine youth, excited his pity. Listening to the truth, he took home the innocent victims of perfidy, and retaliated upon the traducer by hanging him from the highest tower of his castle. After her death, the countess became St. Genofeva, and is the patroness of the parish church of St. Genevieve, which is a lofty structure with four towers which rise high above the surrounding buildings in a fashion which would be truly imposing were the church less overornamented in all its parts.

GENERAL VIEW OF ANDERNACH

The actual foundation of the church dates from Carlovingian times, and a tenth-century church is visibly incorporated into the present fabric, but in the main the present structure is of the thirteenth century.

The façade, as is the case with most of the Romano-Byzantine churches on the Rhine, is flanked by two fine towers, showing some slight traces of the incoming ogival style.

Flanking the apside are two other towers, somewhat heavier and thoroughly Romanesque in motive.

The southern doorway is surrounded by a series of remarkably elaborate and excellent sculptures, showing delicate foliage, birds, and human figures disposed after the best manner of the Romanesque. The northern doorway is decorated in a similar manner, with an elaborate grouping of two angels and the paschal lamb in the tympanum. To the right of this portal is a curious coloured bas-relief set in the wall. It represents the death of the Virgin, and dates from the early sixteenth century.

The interior is divided into three naves by two ranges of pillars, square and very short. The arcades between the aisles and the nave are rounded, but the vaulting is ogival.

The second range of pillars forms an arcade quite similar to the lower one, but the pillars are of black marble. A modern balustrade, which has been added, is frightful in its contrast with the more ancient constructive details.

Above all are six windows on a side, which in plan and proportions resemble those of the side aisles.

The choir is in effect a cul-de-four, and is lighted by five windows placed rather high up. Below are a series of niches, in which are placed modern statues, about as bad as can be imagined, even in these degenerate architectural times.

The gallery behind the second tier of columns is known as the *mannshaus*, being intended for the male portion of the congregation, the women sitting below.

The pulpit came from the old abbey of Laach.

On the left of the grand nave is the tomb of a knight of Lahnstein, who died in 1541.

There is another legend connected with Andernach which may well be recounted here.

One day, during the minority of the Emperor Henry IV., the tutors of the prince, the proud Archbishop Annon of Cologne and the Palatine, Henry the Furious, held a meeting with certain other seigneurs at Andernach. The same day the inhabitants of Güls, a village near Coblenz, lodged a complaint before the Palatine concerning the exactions of the provost of their village. This last, himself, followed the deputies, magnificently clothed and mounted upon a richly caparisoned horse, counting upon his presence to counteract the impression they might make. Among the collection of wild beasts which had been gathered together for the amusement of the princes was a ferocious bear. When the provost passed near him, the animal sprang upon him and tore him to pieces, whereupon it was supposed that the venerable archbishop had exercised a divine power, and delivered up the oppressor to the fury of a wild beast. Like most of the Rhine legends, it is astonishingly simple in plot, and likewise has a religious turn to it, which shows the great respect of the ancient people of these regions toward their creed.

SINZIG CHURCH

Sinzig

Between Andernach and Bonn is the tiny city of Sinzig, famous for two things,—its charmingly disposed parish church and the wines of Assmanhaus.

The town was the ancient Sentiacum of the Romans, constructed in all probability by Sentius, one of the generals of Augustus.

The church at Sinzig, in company with St. Quirinus at Neuss, has some of the best mediæval glass in Germany.

This small, but typically Rhenish, parish church has also a series of polychromatic decorations which completely cover its available wall space.

There is a vividness about them which may be pleasing to some, but which will strike many as being distinctly unchurchly.

As a Christian edifice, the church at Sinzig, with its central tower and spire, is only remarkable as typifying the style of Romano-ogival architecture which developed so broadly in the Rhine valley at the expense of the purer Gothic.

CHAPTER XXII

TRÈVES

Southwesterly from Coblenz, between the Rhine and Metz, is Trèves, known by the Germans as Trier. Situated at the southern end of a charming valley, which more or less closely follows the banks of the Moselle, it has the appearance of being a vast park with innumerable houses and edifices scattered here and there through the foliage. The city contains many churches, of which the cathedral of St. Pierre et Ste. Hélène is the chief.

At one time the *Augusta Trevirorum* of the Romans was "the richest, the most fortunate, the most glorious, and the most eminent of all the cities north of the Alps," said an enthusiastic local historian.

The claim may be disputed by another whose civic pride lies elsewhere, but all know that Trèves, as the flourishing capital of the *Gaulois belges*, actually rivalled Rome itself.

Augustus established a Roman colony here with its own Senate, and many of the Roman emperors of the long line which followed made it their residence during their sojourn in the north.

From the Augusta Trevirorum of the Romans, the city became in time, under the later Empire, Treviri, from which the present nomenclature of Trèves and Trier comes. It was one of the sixty great towns which were taken from the Romans by the Franks and the Alemanni.

The Roman bridge over the Moselle, built probably by Agrippa, existed until the wars of Louis XIV., in 1669, when it was blown up; and all that now remains of the original work are the foundations of the piers, which were built upon anew in the eighteenth century.

As a bishopric, and later as an archbishopric, the see is the most ancient in Germany, having been founded in 327 by the Empress Hélène.

In the twelfth century it became an archbishopric and an electorate, but during the fourteenth century, because of continual struggles between the municipality and the Church, the archbishops removed to Coblenz.

In the cathedral rests the Holy Coat of Trèves, one of the most sacred relics of the Saviour extant, and supposedly the veritable garment worn by him at the crucifixion, — the seamless garment for which the soldiers cast lots (John xix. 23, 24).

When exposed to public view, which ceremony used to take place only once in thirty years, the holy robe is placed upon the high altar, which has previously been dressed for the occasion. The altar is approached by many steps on each side, and there are several steps at intervals in the aisles, so that the appearance of the long line of pilgrims on their way down the side aisles and up to the altar is most picturesque. As many as twenty thousand pilgrims are said to have paid their devotions to this relic in a single day. They come in processions of hundreds, and sometimes thousands; and are of all classes, but mostly peasants. The lame, the blind, and the sick are included in their ranks, and it is noticeable that the majority are women. They are constantly arriving, pouring in at several gates of the city in an almost continual stream, accompanied by priests, banners, and crosses, and alternately singing and praying. There are many of them heavily laden, their packs on their backs, their bright brass pans, pitchers, and kettles of all shapes in their hands, or slung on their arms, while their fingers are busily employed with their beads. Wayworn and footsore, fatigued and hungry, they yet pursue their toilsome march, intent upon the attainment of the one object of their pilgrimage. It is curious and picturesque to see their long lines of processions in the open country, wending their slow way over the hills, and to hear their hymns, mellowed by distance into a pleasant sound across the broad Rhine. From Germany, Belgium, Holland, France, Hungary, and even Switzerland and Italy they come, and during the whole of their journeys the pilgrims sing and pray almost continually. The accomplishment of their pilgrimages entitles them, by payment of a small offering, to certain absolutions and indulgences. The pure-minded peasant girl seeks remission of sins, the foodless peasant a liberty to eat what the expenses of this pilgrimage will perhaps deprive him of the means of obtaining. The city is literally packed with pilgrims, and the scene in the market-place at nightfall is in the highest degree interesting and picturesque.

"The Holy Coat of Trèves" is a simple tunic, apparently of linen or cotton, of a fabric similar to the closely woven mummy-cloth of the Egyptians. Undoubtedly it is of great antiquity, which many sacred *reliques* may or may not be, judging from their appearances. In appearance it is precisely the same as is that worn by the modern Arab.

This form of tunic, then, has come down from the ages with but little change in the fashions, and seems to be worn by all classes in the East. In colour the relic may originally have been blue, though now of course it is much faded; in fact, is a rusty brown.

TRÈVES CATHEDRAL

The history of this holy robe, according to a Professor Marx, who wrote an account of it which had the approval of the Archbishop of Trèves, is authenticated as far back as 1157 by written testimony, it having been mentioned as then existing in the cathedral of Trèves by Frederick I. in a letter addressed to Hillen, Archbishop of Trèves in that year. Its earliest history depends wholly on tradition, which says that it was obtained by the Empress Hélène in the year 326, while in the Holy Land, whither she went for the express purpose of obtaining relics of our Saviour and his followers; that she gave it to the see of Trèves, and that it was deposited in the cathedral of that city; that it was afterward lost, having been hidden in disturbed times within the walls of the cathedral, and rediscovered under the Archbishop John I., in 1196; that it was again hidden for the same reason, brought to light, and exposed to the wondering multitude in 1512, on the occasion of the famous Diet of Trèves, under the Emperor Maximilian. "Since this last epoch," says the author of the work already quoted, "the history of the Holy Robe has been often discussed, written, and sung, because it has been often publicly exposed, and at short intervals, whenever political troubles have not prevented."

At Trèves is an ancient tomb to Cardinal Ivo, with heavily sculptured capitals surmounting four small columns, whose pedestals are crouching lions. But for the crudity of the sculpture, and the weird beasts at its base, one might almost think the tomb a Renaissance work.

The cardinal died in 1142, and the work is unquestionably of the Romanesque period. It is reminiscent, moreover, of the southern portal of the Cathedral of Notre Dame of Embrun in the south of France; indeed, a drawing of one might well pass for the other were it not labelled, though to be sure there is a distinct difference in detail.

Among the treasures of Trèves is a censer, one of the most elaborate ever devised. It is in the form of an ample bowl, with its cover worked in silver in the form of a church on the lines of a Greek cross. The device is most unusual, but rather clumsily ornate.

There are two curious statues in the portal of Notre Dame; one representing the Church and the other the synagogue; the one with a clear, straightforward look in her eyes, the other blindfolded and with the crown falling from her head. The symbol is frequently met with, but the method of indicating the opposition of the new religious law to that of the old is, in these life-size statues, at Trèves, perhaps unique. The figures are somewhat mutilated, each lacking the arms, but in other respects they stand as originally conceived.

The cathedral of St. Pierre et Ste. Hélène is situated in the most elevated portion of the city, and, like the cathedral at Bonn, above Cologne, presents that curious pyramidal effect so often remarked in Rhenish churches.

There is no very great beauty in the outlines of this church, which is a curious jumble of towers and turrets; but there are some very good architectural details, quite worthy of a more splendid edifice. Ste. Hélène, the mother of Constantine, herself placed the first stone in the easterly portion of the present church, a fact which was only discovered in the seventeenth century, when the foundations were being repaired. It is supposed originally to have been a part of the palace of the Empress Hélène, afterward converted into a house of God.

One notes in the interior a remarkably beautiful series of Corinthian columns with elaborately carved capitals of the eleventh century. In later years these have been flanked by supporting pillars which detract exceedingly from the beauty of the earlier forms.

In parts the edifice is frankly French Gothic, Byzantine, and what we know elsewhere as Norman,—a species of the Romanesque.

In 1717 the church suffered considerably by fire, but it was repaired forthwith, and to-day gives the effect of a fairly well cared for building of three naves and a double choir.

There are sixteen altars, some of which are modern, and two organs, cased as usual in hideous mahogany.

The high altar and the pulpit are excellently sculptured, and there are some notable monuments to former archbishops and electors.

Beneath the church are vast subterranean passages, and a great vault where repose the ancient regents of the province.

Architecturally, Trèves's other remarkable church (Notre Dame) quite rivals the cathedral itself in interest. It is one of the best examples of German mediæval architecture extant.

In the year 1227 when St. Géréon's at Cologne, one of the earliest examples of ogival vaulting in Germany, was just finished, there was commenced the church of Notre Dame at Trèves. It was the first church edifice in Germany to consistently carry out the Gothic motive from the foundation stones upward.

For fifty years the well-defined Gothic had been knocking at the gateway which led from France into Germany, and at last it was to enter at a period when the cathedrals at Soissons and Laon had already established themselves as well-nigh perfect examples of the new style.

The first foundation stone was laid in 1227, and the work was completed in less than twenty years. The general plan is grandiose and it has a central cupola—replacing a tower which was in danger of subsiding—held aloft by twelve hardy columns, on which are ranged in symmetrical order statues of the apostles.

The plan is unusual and resembles no Gothic structure elsewhere, hence may be considered as a type standing by itself.

The exterior shows little or nothing of the highly developed Gothic which awaits one when viewing the interior. There are no flying buttresses, the walls seemingly supporting themselves, and yet they are not clumsy. The piers of the chapel somewhat perform the functions of buttresses, and that perhaps makes possible the unusual arrangement.

The church of St. Gangolphe, on the market-place, has a singularly beautiful and very lofty tower, which gives to whoever has the courage to make its rather perilous ascent one of the most charming prospects of the valley of the Moselle possible to imagine.

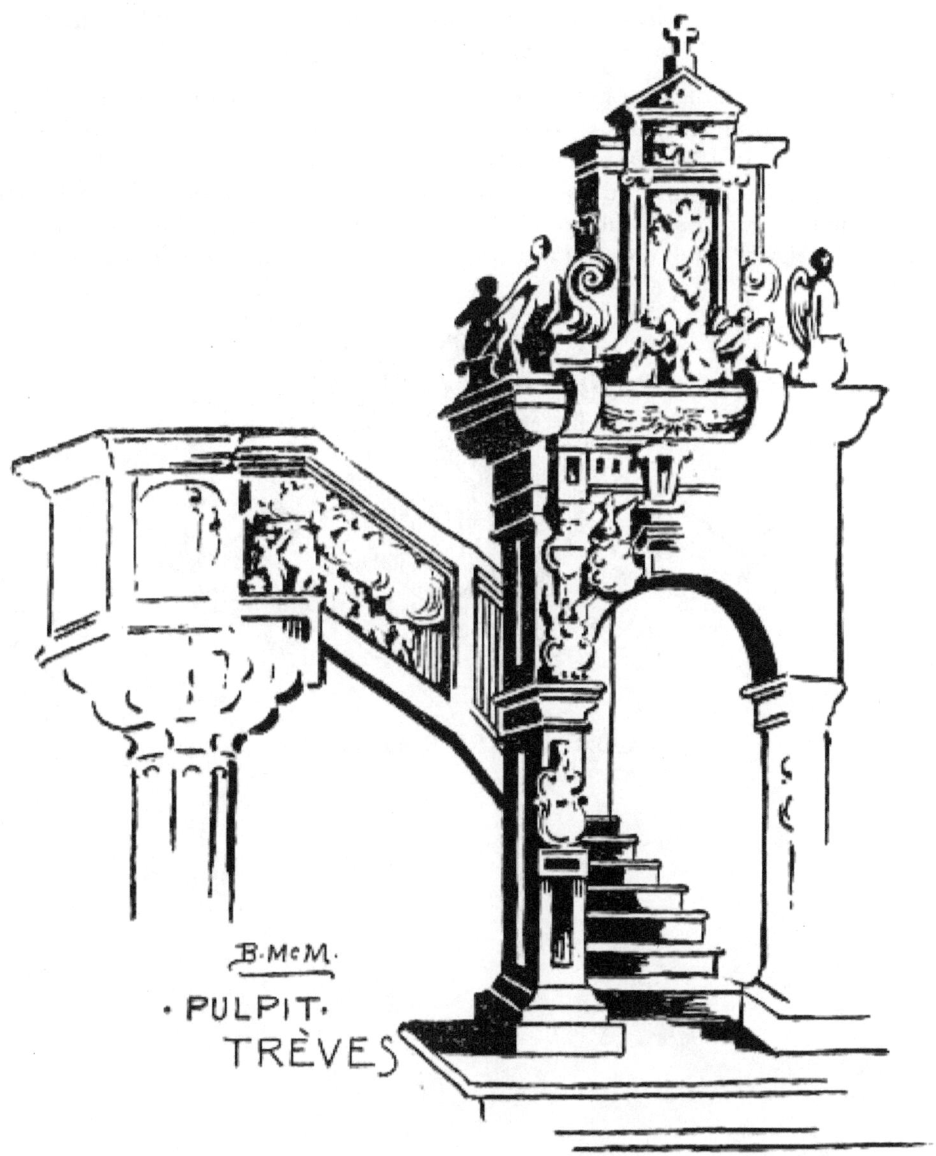

PULPIT, TRÈVES CATHEDRAL

The chief of Trèves's other churches are: the church of the Jesuits, since ceded to the Protestants; St. Gervais, which has a tomb to Bishop Hontheim, a most learned man and a great benefactor of Trèves in days gone by; St. Antoine; and St. Paul.

The country around Trèves, on the Moselle,—the famous Trèves Circle,—

ranks high as a wine-growing region, though your true German wine-drinker calls all Moselle wine "*Unnosel Wein.*"

These wines of the Moselle are, to be sure, secondary to those of the vineyards of the Rhine and the Main, but the varieties are very numerous.

A Dutch burgomaster once bought of the Abbey of Maximinus—a famous wine-growing establishment as well as a religious community—a variety known as Gruenhaüser, in 1793, for eleven hundred and forty-four florins a vat of something less than three hundred gallons. It was known as the nectar of Moselle, and "made men cheerful, and did good the next day, leaving the bosom and head without disorder." Such was the old-time monkish estimate and endorsement of its virtues.

COAT OF ARMS, TRÈVES

CHAPTER XXIII

BONN

Bonn in the popular mind is noteworthy chiefly for its famous university, and for being the birthplace of Beethoven.

The city was one of the fifty fortresses built by Drusus on the Rhine, and the only Rhenish city, with the exception of Cologne, which has kept its Roman appellation. It is mentioned by Tacitus both as *Bonna* and *Bonensia castra*.

The cathedral is as famous as the university. It was funded by the mother of Constantine the Great, who, according to tradition, consecrated the primitive church here in 319.

Really, it is not a very stupendous pile, the present cathedral, but it looks far more imposing than it really is by reason of its massive central tower and steeple.

It is one of the most ancient and most remarkable of the cathedrals on the banks of the Rhine.

The effect of its five towers is that of a great pyramid rising skyward from a broad base.

In the main, it is a construction of the twelfth and thirteenth centuries, but it is known beyond doubt that the choir and the crypt were built in 1157. To-day there are visible no traces of even the foundations of the primitive church.

There are two polygonal apsides, more noticeable from without than within.

The main portal, or the most elaborate at least, is that of the north façade.

The interior is not as sombre and sad as is often the case with a very early church. To enter, one ascends eight steps to the pavement, when the rather shallow vista of the nave and choir opens out broadly.

There are a series of white marble statues representing the birth and baptism of Christ, and some paintings of notable merit, including an "Adoration."

In the crypt, already mentioned, are the bones of the martyrs, Cassius, Florentinus, and Malusius.

The chief interest of the interior, outside of the constructive elements of the fabric, centres in a great statue of St. Hélène in bronze, which is placed in the middle of the grand nave. It is a fine monument, and was cast in the seventeenth century as a somewhat tardy recognition of the founder of the church at Bonn.

GENERAL VIEW OF BONN

APSE, BONN CATHEDRAL

At the western extremity of the nave is the Gothic tomb of Archbishop Englebert, and another of Archbishop Robert.

The choir is somewhat raised above the pavement of the nave, being placed upon the vaulting of the crypt. The walls of the choir are hung with gilded Cordovan leather, which is certainly rich and beautiful, though it has been criticized as being more suitable to a boudoir than a great church.

At the foot of the choir, to the right, is a tabernacle, a feature frequently met with in German churches. It is of Renaissance design and workmanship, and is ungainly and not in the best of taste.

Behind the great pillars of the choir are found, back to back, two imposing altars, to which access is had by mounting a dozen more steps, far above the pavement of the nave. They are most peculiarly disposed, and are again a Renaissance interpolation which might well have been omitted.

In this dimly lighted cathedral, as well as in many other churches of Germany, you may at times hear that hymn known as "Ratisbon," the words of which begin:

> *"Jesus meine Zuversicht*
> *Lebt, und ich soll mit ihm leben."*

There is a legend—or it may be a true tale—connecting these verses with a German soldier who died at the fateful battle of Jena.

Fleeing from the French, he had fallen into the waters of the Saale. Recovering himself, he crawled out, only to find his pursuers on the bank, their firearms levelled at his head. His first thought was to thank God for his safety from the flood, and, kneeling, he played upon his bugle the familiar air to which the hymn, *"Jesus meine Zuversicht,"* is sung. Deeply moved, his pursuers dropped their guns, but, just as the last notes of the tune were dying away, another detachment came up, and one of its members fired a shot which ended the life of the devout Prussian.

There is heard here also a legend, of the time of the Crusades, concerning the Siebengebergen,—the Seven Mountains,—which lie just back of Bonn.

Stimulated by religious fervour, the overlord of a castle perched upon one of the Seven Mountains, enlisted in the army of the Crusaders, and fought gallantly in the very forefront of those who sought to plant the Cross upon the walls of the Holy City. After a prolonged absence, he returned to find that a rival had won the love of his lady, who, to escape his wrath, had fled to a convent.

The usurper of affections escaped, but the injured husband met near Godesberg, in his old age, a youth in whom he thought he recognized the likeness of his wife. Questioning the boy, he visited the sin of the mother upon the child, and slew him on the highroad, on the spot where the Hoch Kreuz now stands,—a monument which tradition says was erected to warn weak wives and faithless friends.

Drachenfels, whose fame to English ears has mostly been made by Byron's verses, lies not far south of Bonn. Byron's "peasant girls with deep blue eyes" are mostly engaged in husbandry to-day, instead of poetically and leisurely gathering "early flowers."

> "The castled crag of Drachenfels
> Frowns o'er the wide and winding Rhine,"

and is still one of the tourist sights of the Rhine, and as such it must be accorded its place.

Bonn was formerly the residence of the Electors of Cologne, after their removal from that city in 1268, at which time it was also the shelter of Archbishop Englebert, who had fled from Cologne.

CHAPTER XXIV

GODESBERG AND ROLANDSECK

Godesberg

WITHIN full view of the Seven Mountains, on the opposite bank of the Rhine, is Godesberg,—"a cheerful village with a castle which is a splendid ruin," say the guide-books.

They might go a bit further and recount something of its political and religious history, although usually they do not, but rush the tourist up-river to Coblenz, giving him only a sort of panoramic view of this portion of the Rhine.

Originally a *castellum romain*, the "cheerful village," known to the ancients as Ara Ubiorum, came under the control, in 1210, of the Archbishop Theodoric of Cologne, who built a chapel to St. Michael on the ancient ruins, which, according to tradition, had endured from the times of Julian the Apostate.

For many centuries there was a château here which served as the country-house of many of the archbishop-electors of the Empire, until destroyed by a thunderbolt. In 1593 it was pillaged by the troops of the Archbishop Ernest, and to-day only a great, lone, round tower remains intact.

For the rest it is a fine ruin and a picturesque one.

Rolandseck

But a short distance above Godesberg is Rolandseck; opposite which is the island of Nonnenwerth, with which it is associated in a famous legend.

The chivalrous Roland sought the love of some fair being, whose beauty and whose virtues should deserve and retain the heart of so brave and gallant a young knight. Nor did he look about in vain, for Hilda, the daughter of the lord of the Drachenfels, was all that dreams had pictured to his youthful fancy as worthy of an ardent soul's devotion, and soon he was made happy by a confession from the maiden that his passion was returned. Lost in a dream of first love, the knight forgot the world and its struggles, and, in the expectation of an early day for his wedding with his mistress, he lived a life of perfect joy,—now gazing with Hilda upon the windings of the Rhine; now watching her as she stooped gracefully to tend the flowers which peace allowed to flourish under the walls of her father's stronghold.

But Roland lived in times when love was but the bright, transient episode of a life of war. The laws of chivalry forbade a true knight's neglect of duty, and, in the very week in which he was to be wedded, the summons came for him to take the field.

The war was long, and it was three years before Roland left the camp. When he reached the home of his mistress, he received a frightful welcome. The castle was in ruins; its lord was slain; and Hilda, deceived by reports of Roland's death, had taken the veil in the neighbouring convent of Nonnenwerth!

CONVENT OF NONNENWERTH

Over the bright path of the young knight a dark and lasting shadow was cast. His early hopes were shattered; the joy of his existence had fled; his spirit bent beneath the weight of his evil fortune. But his faith and constancy were beyond the control of Fate. Retiring to his castle of Rolandseck, he made himself a seat within a window, from which he could look down upon the island of Nonnenwerth and the convent that held his beloved Hilda. Whether she heard of his return tradition does not say; but the rumour of such constancy was perhaps wafted through the nunnery walls. Be that as it may, it is chronicled that, after Roland's watch had been for three years prolonged, he heard one evening the tones of the bell that tolled for a passing soul, and next day the white figures of the nuns were seen bearing a sister to her last home. It was the funeral of Hilda.

The isle of Nonnenwerth and its convent are still there opposite the grim, gaunt, ruined gateway of Rolandseck, a brilliant jewel in an antique setting; and, while neither the conventual buildings nor the ruined château show any unusual architectural features, they are characteristic of the feudal and religious architecture of the middle ages.

Architects of to-day do not build with the same simplicity and grace that they did of old, and these little out-of-the-way gems of architecture are far more satisfying than are similar erections of to-day.

CHAPTER XXV
COLOGNE AND ITS CATHEDRAL

No stranger ever yet entered Cologne without going straight to see its mighty Gothic cathedral. Three things come to him forcibly,—the fact that it was only completed in recent years, the great and undecided question as to who may have been its architect, and the "Legend of the Builder," as the story is known.

There are two legends of the cathedral and its builders which no visitor will ever forget.

The Architect of Cologne

Mighty was Archbishop Conrad de Hochsteden, for he was lord over the chief city of the Rhine, the city of Cologne; but his thoughts were troubled, and his heart was heavy, for, though his churches were rich beyond compare in relics, yet other towns not half so large or powerful as his had cathedrals whose fame extended over Europe, and whose beauty brought pilgrims to their shrines, profit to the ecclesiastics, and business to the townspeople. After many sleepless nights, therefore, he determined to add to his city the only thing wanting to complete it, and, sending for the most famous architect of the time, he commissioned him to draw the plans for a cathedral of Cologne.

Now the architect was a clever man, but he was more vain than clever. He had a vague idea of the magnificence which he desired to achieve without a clear conception of how he was to do it, or without the will to make the necessary sacrifices of labour, care, and perseverance. He received the commission with great gladness, and gloated for some days upon the fame which would be his as the builder of the structure which the archbishop desired; but when, after this vision of glory, he took his crayons to sketch out the design, he was thrown into the deepest despondency. He drew and drew, and added, and erased, and corrected, and began again, but still did not succeed. Not a plan could he complete. Some were too mean, others too extravagant, and others, when done and examined, were found to be good, but not original. Efforts of memory instead of imagination, their points of excellence were but copies of other cathedrals,—a tower from one, a spire from another, an aisle from a third, and an altar from a fourth; and one after another they were cast aside as imperfect and useless, until the draughtsman, more than half-crazed, felt inclined to end his troubles and perplexities by a plunge into the Rhine.

GENERAL VIEW OF COLOGNE

In this mood of more than half-despair, he wandered down to the river's edge, and, seating himself upon a stone, began to draw in the sand with a measuring rod, which served as a walking-stick, the outlines of various parts of a church. Ground-plans, towers, finials, brackets, windows, columns, appeared one after another, traced by the point of his wand; but all, one after another, were erased as unequal and insufficient for the purpose, and unworthy to form a part of the design for a cathedral of Cologne. Turning around, the architect was aware that another person was beside him, and, with surprise, the disappointed draughtsman saw that the stranger also was busily making a design. Rapidly on the sand he sketched the details of a most magnificent building, its towers rising to the clouds, its long aisles and lofty choir stretching away before the eye of the startled architect, who mentally confessed that it was indeed a temple worthy of the Most High. The windows were enriched by tracery such as artist never had before conceived, and the lofty columns reared their tall length toward a roof which seemed to claim kindred with the clouds, and to equal the firmament in expanse and beauty. But each section of this long-sought plan vanished the moment it was seen, and, with a complete conviction of its excellence, the architect was unable to remember a single line.

"Your sketch is excellent," said he to the unknown; "it is what I have thought and dreamed of,—what I have sought for and wished for, and have not been able to find. Give it to me on paper, and I will pay you twenty gold pieces."

"Twenty pieces! ha! ha! twenty gold pieces!" laughed the stranger. "Look here!" and from a doublet that did not seem big enough to hold half the money, he drew forth a purse that certainly held a thousand.

The night had closed in, and the architect was desperate. "If money cannot tempt you, fear shall force you;" and, springing toward the stranger, he plucked a dagger from his girdle, and held its point close to the breast of the mysterious draughtsman. In a moment his wrists were pinioned, as with the grasp of a vise, and squeezed until he dropped his weapon and shrieked in agony. Falling on the sands, he writhed like an eel upon the fisherman's hook; but plunged and struggled in vain. When nearly fainting, he felt himself thrown helpless upon the very brink of the stream.

"There! revive, and be reasonable. Learn that gold and steel have no power over me. You want my cathedral, for it would bring you honour, fame, and profit; and you can have it if you choose."

"How?—tell me how?"

"By signing this parchment with your blood."

"Avaunt, fiend!" shrieked the architect; "in the name of the Saviour I bid thee begone." And so saying, he made the sign of the cross; and the Evil One (for it was he) was forced to vanish before the holy symbol. He had time, however, to mutter: "You'll come for the plan at midnight to-morrow."

The architect staggered home, half-dead with contending passions, and muttering: "Sell my soul," "To-morrow at midnight," "Honour and fame," and other words which told the struggle going on within his soul. When he reached his lodgings, he met the only servant he had going out wrapped in her cloak.

"And where are you going so late?" said her surprised master.

"To a mass for a soul in purgatory," was the reply.

"Oh, horror! horror! no mass will avail me. To everlasting torments shall I be doomed;" and, hurrying to his room, he cast himself down with tears of remorse, irresolution, and despair. In this state his old housekeeper discovered him on her return from her holy errand, and, her soul being full of charity and kindly religion, she begged to know what had caused such grief; and spoke of patience in suffering, and pardon by repentance. Her words fell upon the disordered ear of the architect with a heavenly comfort; and he told her what had passed.

"Mercy me!" was her exclamation. "Tempted by the fiend himself!—so strongly, too!" and, so saying, she left the chamber without another word, and hurried off to her confessor.

Now the confessor of Dame Elfrida was the friend of the abbot, and the abbot was the constant counsellor of the archbishop, and so soon as the housekeeper spoke of the wonderful plan, he told her he would soon see her master, and went at once to his superior. This dignitary immediately pictured to himself the host of pilgrims that would seek a cathedral built with skill from such wonderful sketches, and (hoping himself one day to be archbishop) he hurried off to the bewildered architect.

He found him still in bed, and listened with surprise to the glowing account of the demon's plan.

"And would it be equal to all this?"

"It would."

"Could you build it?"

"I could."

"Would not pilgrims come to worship in such a cathedral?"

"By thousands."

"Listen, my son! Go at midnight to the appointed spot; take this relic with you;" and, so saying, the abbot gave him a bone of one of the Eleven Thousand Virgins. "Agree to the terms for the design you have so long desired, and when you have got it, and the Evil One presents the parchment for your signature, show this sacred bone."

After long pondering, the priest's advice was taken; and, in the gloom of night, the architect hurried tremblingly to the place of meeting. True to his time, the fiend was there, and, with a smile, complimented the architect on his punctuality. Drawing from his doublet two parchments, he opened one, on which was traced the outline of the cathedral, and then another written in some mysterious character, and having a space left for a signature.

"Let me examine what I am to pay so dearly for."

"Most certainly," said the demon, with a smile, and a bow that would have done honour to the court of the emperor.

Pressing it with one hand to his breast, the architect with the other held up the holy bone, and exclaimed: "Avaunt, fiend! In the name of the Father, and the Son, and the Holy Virgins of Cologne, I hold thee, Satan, in defiance;" and he described the sign of the cross directly against the devil's face.

In an instant the smile and the graceful civility were gone. With a hideous grin, Satan approached the sacred miracle as though he would have strangled the possessor; and, yelling with a sound that woke half the sleepers in Cologne, he skipped round and round the architect. Still, however, the plan was held tightly with one hand, and the relic held forward like a swordsman's rapier with the other. As the fiend turned, so turned the architect; until, bethinking himself that another prayer would help him, he called loudly on St. Ursula. The demon could keep up the fight no longer; the leader of the Eleven Thousand Virgins was too much for him.

"None but a confessor could have told you how to cheat me," he shrieked in a most terrible voice; "but I will be revenged. You have a more wonderful and perfect design than ever entered the brain of man. You want fame,—the priest wants a church and pilgrims. Listen! *That cathedral shall never be finished, and your name shall be forgotten!*"

As the dreadful words broke upon the architect's ear, the cloak of the Tempter stretched out into huge black wings, which flapped over the spot like two dark thunderclouds, and with such violence that the winds were raised from their slumber, and a storm rose upon the waters of the Rhine. Hurrying homewards, the relic raised at arm's length over his head, the frightened man reached the abbot's house in safety. But the ominous sentence still rang in his ears,—"*Unfinished and forgotten.*"

Days, months, years passed by, and the cathedral, commenced with vigour, was growing into form. The architect had long before determined that an inscription should be engraved upon a plate of brass shaped like a cross, and be fastened upon the front of the first tower that reached a good elevation. His vanity already anticipated a triumph over the Fiend whom he had defrauded. He was author of a building which the world could not equal, and, in the pride of his heart, defied all evil chances to deprive him of fame. Going to the top of the building to see where his name should be placed, he looked over the edge of the building to decide if it was lofty enough to deserve the honour of the inscription, when the workmen were aware of a black cloud which suddenly enveloped them, and burst in thunder and hail. Looking around, when the cloud had passed away, *their master was gone!* and one of them declared that amidst the noise of the explosion he heard a wail of agony which seemed to say, "*Unfinished and forgotten.*"

When they descended the tower, the body of the architect lay crushed upon the pavement. The traveller who beholds the building knows of the difficulties which beset its completion, and thousands have since then sought in vain to learn the name of "The Architect of Cologne," although of late years—though with some doubt it is stated—his name and fame appear to have been established.

The Pfaffen Thor

When Archbishop Conrad of Hochsteden, the founder of the cathedral, had been gathered to his fathers, Engelbrecht of Falkenberg reigned over Cologne in his stead; and a fearful tyrant he became.

As in the case of the spiritual lords who ruled over Liège, the crozier of the archbishop became a rod of iron to the citizens, until at length they were goaded to open rebellion. In their contests for liberty, they were led by Hermann Grynn, a townsman who had put aside the peaceful pursuit of his trade to do battle in the good cause of his native city, and to maintain the privileges which his fathers had purchased, not only with their gold, but with their blood.

After numerous contests between the burghers and their oppressors, the cause of the many was triumphant, and the archbishop was glad to agree to terms which he before had spurned. But the truce he sought was hollow and unfaithful, and he was heard to say that, if Hermann Grynn were removed, he would be able to take away the privileges he had surrendered to the townsmen.

This treacherous speech was greedily received by two priests, who determined to advance their own welfare by the downfall of the citizen-patriot. Making the acquaintance of Hermann, whose honest nature suspected no treachery, they wormed themselves into his confidence, and at a fitting opportunity invited him to the cathedral to see its hidden beauties and great store of riches. Leading him from chapel to cloister, and through chamber after chamber, they came at length to a door which they said contained the richest sight of all; and one of them, unlocking the door, invited the citizen to enter. No sooner had he crossed the threshold than the thick portal was closed suddenly upon him, and, at the same moment, he heard the roar of some wild animal, and saw fixed upon him two fierce eyes gleaming with hunger and savage rage.

Hermann Grynn was a man for emergencies. Rapidly twisting his cloak around his left arm, and drawing his short sword, he prepared for the attack; nor had he long to wait. With a growl of triumph, a huge animal sprang upon him with open jaws; but with admirable coolness the hero received his assailant upon the guarded arm, and, whilst the brute ground its teeth into the cloak, he thrust his sword into its heart. Searching around the chamber, he was aware of a window concealed by a shutter, and, opening this, he looked forth into the streets, where a great crowd was collected around a priest, who went along telling some tale which seemed to move the people to deep grief. As the throng drew nearer, he listened eagerly, and heard with surprise "how the good burgess Hermann Grynn, the friend of the people, and the well-beloved ally of the Church, had without advice sought a chamber where a lion was in durance, and had fallen a sacrifice to his unhappy curiosity." Burning with rage and a determination to expose the treachery of the priests, he waited till the crowd came beneath the window from which he looked; and then, dashing the glass into a thousand pieces, he attracted attention to the spot, and, leaning half out of the opening, displayed his well-known cap in one hand and his bloody sword in the other. He was almost too high to be heard, but the faint echo of his war-cry was enough to convince the people of his identity, and with one voice they shouted: "To the rescue!" Forcing their way into the cathedral, they quickly released their leader, and, learning from him the story of cruel treachery, the two priests were ferreted from their hiding-places, and hanged by the neck in the room over the body of the dead lion. To this day the portal they slammed on Hermann Grynn is known as the *Pfaffen Thor*,—the priest's door,—whilst over the gate of the venerable town hall of Cologne may yet be seen, graven in stone, the fight of the citizen-patriot with the hungry lion of the cathedral.

These two legends refer solely to the cathedral. There is, in addition, the rather more familiar one of "St. Ursula and the Eleven Thousand Virgins."

And, besides legends, there is much real symbolism that peeps out wherever one turns. The skulls of the "Three Kings" still grin from under their crowns in the cathedral, as they did when Frederick Barbarossa stormed Milan and brought back these relics of the three *Magi*. Beneath the pavement of the cathedral lies buried the heart of Marie de Medici, who, in her fallen fortunes, died at Sternen-Gasse 10, in the house where Peter Paul Rubens was born.

In a rather roundabout way the name of one great in letters is associated with Cologne. Petrarch came here on his way from Avignon to Paris in 1331, and the superb beginnings of the new cathedral inspired him with the most profound admiration. In a letter which he addressed to his friend and protector, Jean Colonna, he said: "I have seen in this city the most beautiful temple; yet incomplete, but which is truly entitled to rank as a supreme work."

It was a fortunate day for the history of the church at Cologne when the Evangelist first preached the gospel in the city of Colonia Agrippina. In those days the primitive church sheltered itself modestly under the shadow of the Roman fortress, whereas to-day the great cathedral rises, stately and proud, high above the fortification of the warlike Teuton—if he really be warlike, as the statesmen of other nations proclaim.

When Charlemagne fixed his official residence at Aix-la-Chapelle, he placed his imperial palace in the diocese of Cologne; the two cities together, by reason of their power and importance, standing as a symbol of mightiness which did much to make the great, unwieldy dominion of the Carlovingian Emperor hang together.

It has been claimed, and there certainly seems some justification for it, that the general plan of the cathedral at Cologne is similar to that of Notre Dame d'Amiens; there is something about the general scale and proportions that makes them quite akin. Perhaps this is due to the particularly daring combination of its lines and the general hardiness of its plan and outline. These features are certainly common to both in a far greater degree than are usually found between two such widely separated examples. At any rate, it is perhaps as safe a conjecture as any, since the hand that traced the plan of Cologne is lost in doubtful obscurity, to consider that there is something more than an imaginary bond between the cathedrals of Amiens and Cologne.

A resemblance still more to be remarked is the great height of the choir and nave. This is most marked at Amiens and still more so at Beauvais. Cologne, as to these dimensions, ranks between the two.

There was once a Romanesque cathedral at Cologne, but a fire made way with it in 1248. Certain facts have come down to us regarding this earlier building, but they appear decidedly contradictory, though undoubtedly it was an edifice of the conventional Rhenish variety. It is supposed that this original cathedral had at least a "family resemblance" to those at Mayence, Worms, and Speyer.

These three great ecclesiastical works in the Rhine valley mark the Hohenstaufen dynasty as one of the most prolific in German church-building. Although they are not as beautiful as one pictures the perfect cathedral of his imagination, — at least no more beautiful than many other hybrid structures, — they show an individuality that is peculiarly Rhenish, far more so than the present cathedral at Cologne or any of the smaller churches of the region.

After the fire in 1248 a new cathedral was planned as a commensurate shrine in which to shelter the relics of the "Three Wise Men of the East," which henceforth were to be known as "The Three Kings of Cologne." From this period on, Cologne began to acquire such wealth and prominence as to mark the era as the "Golden Age" in the civic and ecclesiastical affairs of the city.

Abandoning the *basilica* plan entirely, a great Gothic church was undertaken. In its way it was to rival those Gothic masterpieces of France.

The origin of the plan of the cathedral in fact, as well as in legend, is vague. Some have considered Archbishop Engelbert, Count of Altona and Berg, who was murdered in 1225, as the author, but this can hardly have been so, unless it were conceived before the *basilica* was burned.

Assiduous research has been made from time to time in an effort to discover the identity of the actual designer of the present cathedral: Archbishops Engelbert and Conrad, Albertus Magnus, Meister Gerard, and others have all had the honour somewhat doubtfully awarded to them and again withdrawn.

There is a great painting exhibited at Frankfort called "Religion Glorified by the Arts," by Overbeck, wherein is an ideal portrait of the "Great Unknown of Cologne" pictured as the genius of architecture.

A comparatively recent discovery seems to award the honour to Gerard de St. Trond. A charter of 1257 makes mention of the fact that the chapter of the cathedral had given a house, for services rendered, to one Gerard, "a stone-cutter," who had directed the work of construction; this gift being made some years after the foundations were first laid.

The same architect figures among the benefactors of the hospital of St. Ursula as "the master of the works at the cathedral." Perhaps, then, the name of Gerard de St. Trond deserves to be placed with that of Libergier, the designer of Reims, the greatest Gothic splendour of France.

Engelbert's successor, Conrad of Hochsteden, furthered the plans, whoever may have been their creator, and work on the new edifice was begun a few months after the destruction of the older one.

On August 14, 1248, the foundation-stone of the new structure was laid, forty-four feet below the surface of the ground.

The portion first erected was the choir, and for ages it stood, as it stands in its completed form to-day, as perfect an example of the style of its period as is extant.

For seventy years this choir was taking form, until it was consecrated on September 27, 1322.

The occasion was a great one for Cologne and for the church. The ceremony was attended by much glitter and pomp, both ecclesiastical and civil.

No sooner was the choir completed than it was embellished as befitted the shrine of the three kings.

Coloured glass, stone, and wood-carving, and the art of the gold and jewel smith all blended to give a magnificence to the whole which was perhaps unapproachable elsewhere at the time.

Then, for a time, enthusiasm and labour languished. For nearly two centuries the work was pursued by the prelates and architects in a most desultory and intermittent fashion.

The choir had been completed, and to the westward considerable progress had been made, but there was a gaunt ugly gap between. It would seem as though there were no intention of ever joining the scattered parts, which were linked only by the foundation-stones, for the nave and aisles were left merely covered with temporary roofs.

Then the Reformation came, and that boded no good for the cathedral. The people looked askance at the symbol of such great power in the hands of Rome.

The seventeenth century saw some abortive efforts toward completing the structure, but in the end all came to nought.

In the eighteenth century the choir received its baptism of the Renaissance, and certain incongruous Italian details were added. The stone screens which surrounded the choir proper were demolished and the painted glass of the triforium mysteriously disappeared.

During the French Revolution, Republican troops bivouacked within the walls of Cologne's cathedral, and the chapter fled to Westphalia, leaving behind valuable archives which were destroyed.

The very fact of its profanation may have been the cause which hastened the restoration of the edifice.

Napoleon himself was deeply moved by the state of the *"ruine pittoresque,"* and, upon the advice of an agent of his government, made a somewhat fitful attempt toward putting it in order. Thus the impetus for the work of restoration and completion was given.

After Napoleon had restored the churches of Cologne to their rightful guardians, he transferred the archbishopric to Aix-la-Chapelle, and Bertholet, the new bishop, contemptuously told the people of Cologne to beautify their ruin by planting trees on its site.

The neglect to which the choir had fallen was shocking, and it took an immediate expenditure on the part of the citizens of over thirty thousand marks to merely repair the leaks in its roof. Tom Hood, a supposed humourist, but in reality a sad soul, wailed over Cologne's cathedral when he saw it in the early years of the nineteenth century, and called it "a broken promise to God"; and Wordsworth wrote of it thus:

> "Oh! for the help of angels to complete
> This temple—Angels governed by a plan
> Thus far pursued (how gloriously!) by man."

A rearrangement of the Catholic sees of Germany took place in 1821, and the archbishopric of Cologne was refounded and Count Charles Spiegel zum Desenburg was appointed archbishop.

COLOGNE CATHEDRAL IN 1820

At this time, also, was undertaken the repair and completion of the cathedral, and thus what had long been a ruin and an unfinished thing was in a fair way to be speedily completed.

The rebuilding of the choir stimulated the desire to carry the entire work to a finish, and a sort of second foundation-stone was laid by Frederick William IV. of Prussia on September 4, 1842, when the newly restored choir was also reopened.

In 1848 the nave had sufficiently progressed to allow of its being consecrated; which ceremony took place at seven o'clock in the morning of August 14th, six hundred years after the commencement of the choir. High mass was celebrated by the archbishop, in the presence of Archduke John, King Frederick William of Prussia, and a host of other notables.

Within the next twenty years much progress was made in the work of completing the southern nave, the west front—with those enormous pretentious towers—the transepts, and the triforium and clerestory of the nave and transepts.

In 1863 the wall between the fragmentary nave and the choir was removed and the structure opened from end to end.

Before 1870 the western towers were spired, though the final touches were not given to them until quite 1880. Now that they are finished, there is an undeniable elegance and symmetry which cannot be gainsaid, though they were certainly heavily massed in the early views one sees of the cathedral in its unfinished state. One still remarks the apparent—and real—stubbiness of the edifice which, as Fergusson said, would have been alleviated if the overhanging transepts had been omitted. Why they should have been omitted it is hard to conceive, and the criticism does not seem a reasonable one, in spite of the fact that a certain sense of length is wanting.

The nave is undoubtedly very broad, but it has double aisles which satisfactorily accounts for this.

Professor Freeman draws a significant contrast between the outline of the cathedrals at Cologne and Amiens.

"Amiens has no outline," says he; meaning that there is a paucity of the picturesqueness of irregularity in its sky-line. "Only at Cologne," he continues, "is this outline seen in its perfect state, and Cologne is a French church on German soil, just as Westminster is a French church on English soil."

Indeed, among all the great cathedrals it is only at Cologne that we find a pair of western towers with any kind of dignity and proportion.

The west front of Cologne is pretty much all tower, with the nave rather rudely crowded between the two. These towers are in reality of such vast bulk that they outflank the nave considerably, as do their smaller counterparts at Wells, though here at Cologne the great transepts overflow the width even of these great towers of the façade.

There is a noble simplicity and yet a wealth of warmth and feeling in this church, which runs the whole gamut of Gothic, from the thirteenth to the sixteenth centuries. From this latter date, however, the style did not change, but was carried out with that devotion to the original plan which should have inspired the imitators of Gothic in our own time to have done better than they have.

The clerestoried choir of Cologne more nearly follows the French variety than does any other in Germany; indeed no other in Germany in any way approaches the dignity and harmony of those magnificent *chevets* which the French builders, for a hundred years before Cologne, had so proudly reared.

Metz in a way also reflects the same motive, though that cathedral in many other respects is French.

The apside is supported by twenty-eight flying buttresses, which again are an echo from France; this time of Beauvais; and certainly, if they do not excel the French type, they at least quite rival it in beauty and grace.

One enters through a magnificently planned vestibule and comes at once, not into darkness, but into a subdued and religious atmosphere which is quite in keeping with the spirit of devotion.

There are numerous monuments scattered about, and there are eight fifteenth-century tapestries from the Gobelins' factory.

The organ-case is unusually ornate and dates from 1572.

The pulpit is not perhaps so elaborate as one might expect from the general splendour surrounding it, but its sculpture is distinctly good.

In the choir, on the screens above the stalls, is a series of restored frescoes which came to light after a coating of whitewash had been removed. They were admirably restored by Steinle in the mid-nineteenth century and are very beautiful. The decorations depict scenes from the life of the Virgin and are also reproduced in part in the glass of the lady-chapel.

A modern altar, in the mediæval style, has replaced the seventeenth-century Renaissance work, which is manifestly for the better, judging from the old engravings that one sees of the former unlovely altar.

The glass throughout is hardly of the excellence that one might expect, but the effect is undeniably good. A portion of that in the Chapel of the Three Kings is a relic of the old Romanesque cathedral, while that of the north aisle of the nave dates from the time of Dürer.

That of the windows of the Chapel of the Three Kings has been called one of the most beautiful pages out of the book of the fifteenth-century glass-worker. The subject referred to is, of course, "The Adoration of the Magi."

The capitals of the columns of the nave and choir are superbly foliaged, and add much to the general sumptuous appearance of the interior.

Before the Chapel of the Three Kings are many tombs; the most remarkable being that which covered the remains of Marie de Medici, who died in exile at Cologne in 1642. One knows that after the death of the crafty Richelieu the body of the queen was transported to St. Denis, there to rest with others of the long line of kings and queens there buried, but the heart remained at Cologne, and, next to the relics of the Three Kings, it is the chief "sight" of interest to inquisitive tourists.

The casket in which repose the relics of the Three Magi is a masterwork of the goldsmith's art of the twelfth century. Incrusted on its surface were more than fifteen hundred precious jewels, although some have disappeared in the course of the ages. Among them is a topaz of monstrous size, which excites the admiration of all who set eyes upon it.

In 1794 the canons transported the casket to Arnsberg, to Prague, and to Frankfort, their financial difficulties of the time forcing them to sell the crowns with which the skulls were adorned. Since then other coronets have replaced the first, set with gems and stones brought from Bohemia.

On the 23d July, 1164, these relics were first deposited in the ancient cathedral, from which they were subsequently transferred to the new edifice amid much ceremony.

In their first resting-place they were guarded only by a simple iron grille up to the time when the archbishop Maximilian Henry constructed the *ædicule* which encloses them to-day.

On the pediment of this screen is sculptured an "Adoration of the Magi," by Michel Van der Voorst of Antwerp. There are also figures of St. Felix and St. Nabor, and two female figures bearing the arms of the Metropolitan Chapter.

On the frieze is the following inscription:

TRIBUS AB ORIENTE REGIBUS
DEVICTO IN AGNITIONE VERI NUMINIS
MUNDO
CAPITULUM METROPOL EREXIT.

And above the great window, whose grille is opened on ceremonial occasions to allow the public a better view of the relics, is graven the following:

CORPORA SANCTORUM RECUBANT HIC
TERNA MAGORUM
EX HIS SUBLATUM NIHIL EST ALIBIVE
LOCATUM.

Finally one reads the following single line placed between the columns at the right and left of the relics:

"Et apertis thesauris suis, obtulerunt munera."

Behind the reliquary which encloses the skulls is a bas-relief in marble representing the solemn journey by which the relics were first brought from Milan. A bas-relief in bronze, richly gilded, represents an "Adoration." It was the gift of Jacques de Croy, Duc de Cambrai, in 1516. The window above contains some fine glass of the thirteenth century.

Before the high altar are four great candelabra of reddish copper, cast at Liège in 1770.

The sculptured stalls of wood, which range themselves in a double row in the choir, are notable for the profusion of figures of men and animals which they show in their carving. They are perhaps not comparable with the stalls at Amiens and at Antwerp, nor with those in Ste. Cécile at Albi in France; but they merit, nevertheless, a very high rank for excellence, and are very extensive as to size and number.

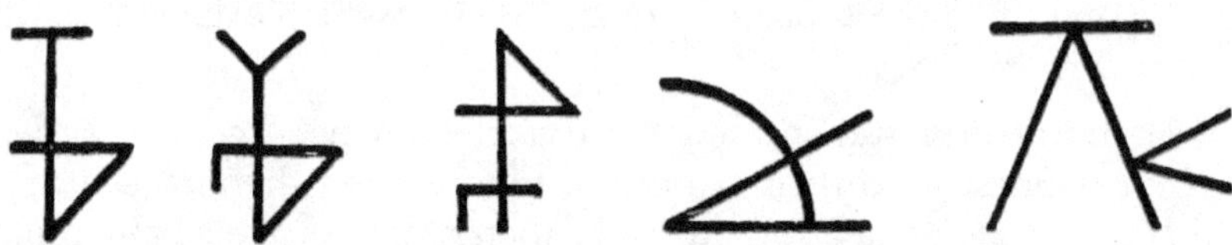

STONE-MASONS' MARKS, COLOGNE CATHEDRAL

To sum up, the cathedral at Cologne has had the good fortune to have been carried out in a pure and distinct German form of Gothic without the interpolation of any *outré* disfigurements. It is a sumptuous edifice, perhaps the grandest, in general effect, of any church in Europe, not even forgetting the splendid cathedrals at Reims, Amiens, or Chartres, all of which stand out from among their surroundings in much the same imposing manner as does Cologne.

One recognizes even to-day on the stones of Cologne's cathedral certain cryptogramic marks which are supposed to be merely the identifying marks of some particular stonemason's labour, and are not, as has been doubtfully advanced from time to time, of any other significance whatever.

COAT OF ARMS, COLOGNE

CHAPTER XXVI

THE CHURCHES OF COLOGNE

THE popular interest in Cologne, the ancient *Colonia Agrippina* of the Romans, and the romantic incidents connected with it, are so great that one might devote a large volume to the city, and then the half of its legend and history would not have been told.

Cologne is one of the most ancient cities of Germany. It takes its place beside Trèves and Mayence as one of the earliest seats of Christianity; but the actual date of the establishment of the church in Cologne is lost in obscurity.

There were undoubtedly persons professing the Christian faith in the colony in the third century, and toward the year 312 the Emperor Constantine, having embraced the faith himself, gave his protection to its adherents throughout his colonies.

The church of St. Peter at Cologne contains a painting presented to it by Rubens in memory of the fact that he was baptized before the altar of this church. Of this picture, a "Crucifixion of St. Peter," Sir Joshua Reynolds wrote:

"It was painted a little time before Rubens's death. The body and head of the saint are the only good parts in this picture, which, however, is finely coloured and well drawn; but the figure bends too suddenly from the thighs, which are ill drawn, or, rather, in a bad taste of drawing; as is likewise his arm, which has a short interrupted outline. The action of the malefactors has not that energy which he usually gave to his figures. Rubens, in his letters to Gildorp, expresses his own approbation of this picture, which he says was the best he ever painted; he likewise expresses his content and happiness in the subject, as being picturesque; this is likewise natural to such a mind as that of Rubens, who was perhaps too much looking about him for the picturesque, or something uncommon. A man with his head downwards is certainly a more extraordinary object than if the head were in its natural place. Many parts of this picture are so feebly drawn, and with so tame a pencil, that I cannot help suspecting that Rubens died before he had completed it, and that it was finished by some of his scholars."

St. Maria in Capitola, one of Cologne's famous churches, stands on the site of the ancient capital of the Romans. It is one of the most perfect examples extant of a triapsed church, though the three apses themselves are supposed to have been an afterthought added in the twelfth century, whereas the nave dates from the century before. The nave, too, has an interpolation or addition to its original form in that a Gothic roof was added some three hundred years after it had first been covered with a plain wooden ceiling.

The three apses unfold grandly, with the high altar in the most easterly or middle termination.

The general effect of the interior is decidedly high coloured, with much polychromatic decoration and painted glass. In the Hardenrath chapel are found the most striking of these mural decorations, which are interesting as illustrating a certain phase of art, if not for their supreme excellence.

St. Pantaleon's claims to be the most ancient church in the city, dating as far back as A. D. 980, when it was reared from the stones of the Roman bridge which before that time stretched across to Deutz. The chapel of the *Minorites* contains the tomb of Duns Scotus, and a horrible tale is told of his entombment alive, of his revival in his coffin, his struggle to escape, and his body being found afterward at the closed door of the sepulchre, with the hand eaten off by himself ere he died of hunger.

FONT, ST. MARTIN'S, COLOGNE

A peculiarity of Cologne's churches—for it is possessed by the Apostles' Church, St. Cunibert's, and St. Andrew's—is the western apse.

Such a member is not unique to Cologne, for it exists in the cathedral at Nevers, in France, and there are yet other examples in Germany; but its use is sufficiently uncommon to warrant speculation as to its purpose.

The Apostles' Church has this feature most highly developed. The edifice is a noble pile dating from early in the eleventh century, but reconstructed two centuries later, to which period it really belongs so far as its general characteristics are concerned.

Not all the church architecture of Cologne is Gothic; indeed the churches of the Apostles and St. Martin each show the Lombard influence to a marked degree. The three apses, and their round arches and galleries, are like a bit of Italy transported northward.

GROSS ST. MARTIN, COLOGNE

St. Maria in Capitola, founded by the wife of Pepin, has the same characteristics, while St. Martin has the outline of quite the ideal Romanesque church. Its great tower, which fills the square between the apses, is certainly one of the most beautiful to be seen on a long round of European travel. This tower must date from the latter years of the twelfth century, and yet, although of a period contemporary with the Gothic of Notre Dame de Paris, it is so thoroughly Romanesque that one wonders that, in Cologne at least, the style ever died out as it did when the great Gothic cathedral was conceived.

St. Andrews is another triapsed church, and is considered one of the best and most elaborately designed fabrics of the Romanesque type on the Rhine, particularly in respect to its central tower, the nave, and the west transept.

There has been much late Gothic rebuilding, but the chief characteristics of the earlier period distinctly predominated. The apses are polygonal, but it is thought that they may, in earlier times, have been semicircular like St. Martin's, St. Mary's, and the Apostles' Churches.

St. Gérêon's is an octagonal church similar to that of Charlemagne at Aix-la-Chapelle. Even more than the latter it has been altered, rebuilt, and added to, but the original outline is still readily traced in spite of the fact that its foundations may have come down from the fifth century. It is more difficult, however, to follow its evolution in detail than it is in the case of Charlemagne's shrine at Aix-la-Chapelle.

The style is distinctly Rhenish, though not alone in Germany do such round churches exist; one recalls the Templars' Church in London and the famous example at Ravenna in Italy.

The great decagon of St. Gérêon's is covered with a domed roof, also divided into ten sections by groins or ribs, which rise gracefully from the slender shafts at the angles, meeting at the apex in a boss.

The ancient collegiate buildings which formerly surrounded St. Gérêon's have disappeared, but there is yet an extensive structure of a more modern date which enfolds the central pile. The easterly apse is low and rectangular, while the façade of the west is flanked by two Romanesque unspired towers.

St. Gérêon's is one of the most curiously constructed churches of the middle ages. It was founded by the Empress Hélène in honour of the Théban martyrs, who, to the number of three hundred and ninety-five, died for their faith, with their captains, Gérêon and Gregory, toward the end of the third century, in the reign of the Emperor Diocletian.

One enters by a rectangular porch, where are disposed some fragments of Roman remains. The rotunda, or decagon, so reminiscent of Aix-la-Chapelle, dates from a period contemporary therewith, so far as its lower walls are concerned, but the upper portions are of the twelfth century, at least.

Below the arches are the chapels which surround the decagon in symmetrical fashion. Above is the organ and the adjoining choir walls. In the latter are walled up innumerable skulls of the companions of St. Gérêon, and in each of the chapels is a great sarcophagus, also containing the bones of the martyrs. Altogether the thought which arises is not a pleasant one, no matter how worthy the object of preserving such a vast quantity of human remains.

ST. GÉRÊON'S, COLOGNE

The high altar is quite isolated, and the pavement of the choir itself, which is aisleless, rises behind it to a height of a dozen or more steps,—a frequent occurrence in the Rhine churches.

The apse has an insertion of Gothic windows, but the eleventh-century Romanesque features are still prominent.

In the choir are a series of flamboyant Gothic stalls, above which are monumental tablets let into the wall.

At the entrance of the choir are two colossal statues of the martyred saints, then seven others, behind which, at the base of the apside, is another altar.

The tapestries which surround the choir are of the *"haut-lisse"* weaving, and represent the life history of Joseph.

Beneath the choir is a vast, antique crypt, which contains yet other sarcophagi filled, presumably, with human bones. The pavement is composed of fragments of antique mosaic.

The Jesuit church at Cologne is one of the few Renaissance examples on the Rhine. It is, however, most unchurchly, when judged by French standards.

Certainly this German example is highly beautiful both in design and execution; but it is not churchly, and its great cylindrical columns, strung together by a gallery, give the appearance of a foyer in an opera-house or of a modern railway-station, rather than that of a place of worship.

It is all nave; there are no transepts, and there is no choir properly speaking, but merely a chancel, not very deep and again very unchurchly, with two ugly lights on either side, and a sort of pagoda-like screen which is decidedly theatrical. The carving of the pulpit and the disposition of all the decoration is extremely bizarre, but undeniably excellent in execution.

Cologne is an archbishopric which has for suffragan sees, Trèves, Münster, and Paderborn.

The abbeys and churches which were erected in Cologne, when the archbishop first took up his residence there in the latter part of the eighth century, were numerous and exceedingly rich in endowment. So much was this so that Cologne was given the name of the "Holy City of the north."

The Jews of Cologne were a numerous body, but a decree of 1425 drove them all from the city. In 1618 a new decree likewise expelled the Protestants. Time regulated all this, but in those days Cologne clung proudly to the position which she had attained as a champion of the orthodox religion.

In all, there were two abbeys, two collegiate churches, the cathedral, forty-nine chapels, thirty-nine monasteries, two convents for women, and many commanderies of the Teutonic order and the Order of Malta.

Near Cologne is the fine old Cistercian abbey of Altenburg. It contains some very ancient coloured glass, perhaps the most beautiful of its era extant, for it is thought to date from between 1270 and 1300, when the art first attained any great excellence.

That which remains to-day shows foliage and diaper in great variety, with no figures whatever, this being a distinct tenet of the Cistercian builders, who, in the severity of their rule, frowned down all decorative effects that bordered upon the frivolous.

These windows at Altenburg, being the best examples of their kind, are the distinct artistic attraction of the great abbey, which is a dozen or more miles distant from Cologne.

The choir was commenced in 1255 and completed almost immediately; but the entire main fabric was not finished until well on in the century following.

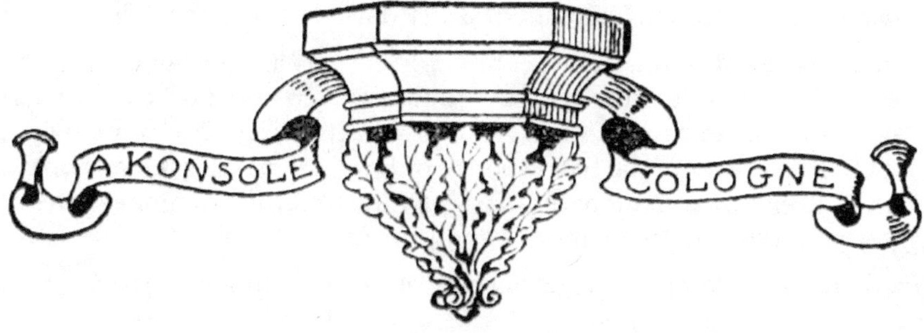

COAT OF ARMS, COLOGNE

CHAPTER XXVII

AIX-LA-CHAPELLE

As Rouen in Normandy was known as "the city of the Conqueror," so Aix-la-Chapelle became known, at a much earlier date, as "the city of Charlemagne."

Charlemagne was more than a conqueror; he was a statesman, with a boundless ambition. He founded the German Empire, and changed tribes of lawless barbarians into a civilized people. At Aix-la-Chapelle he received the embassies of the Caliph of Baghdad and of the Saxon Kings of England, and there he endeavoured to advance the enlightenment of his people by the founding of monasteries and by giving very material aid to the monks and priests.

Aix therefore became the scene of some of the most interesting episodes in the life and career of Charlemagne.

At the death of his consort, Frastrade, Charlemagne was inconsolable. Even when she had been dead for three weeks, the monarch would not hear her death spoken of. "She did but sleep," he said; and the Emperor clung to the chamber of his beloved, and would not abate his watchfulness "till Frastrade woke."

Meantime the affairs of the Empire were falling into confusion. Provinces were all but revolting, and foreign foes were mustering their forces. The Emperor's chief counsellor was the Archbishop of Reims. One night—though this is more legendary than historical—the archbishop was walking by himself when he came upon a shape in the moonlight which proclaimed itself as follows: "I am the good genius of Charlemagne. I came to teach you how to remove the shadow from his spirit. Dig, where I stand, a grave and let the festering body of Frastrade lie in it. But, mark you! Ere you move her body, search beneath her tongue and take out what you find there."

The archbishop hurried toward a grotesquely carved cottage door where lived a gravedigger.

> "No silken sleeper so calm as they
> Who seek a couch in the churchyard clay,"

sang a voice from within.

In half an hour the grave was begun, and in another half-hour the churchman was in the chamber of Frastrade, where the Emperor, exhausted by his vigil, slept kneeling at the bedside.

The archbishop approached, and, peering into the mouth of the corpse, saw beneath the tongue a glittering jewel.

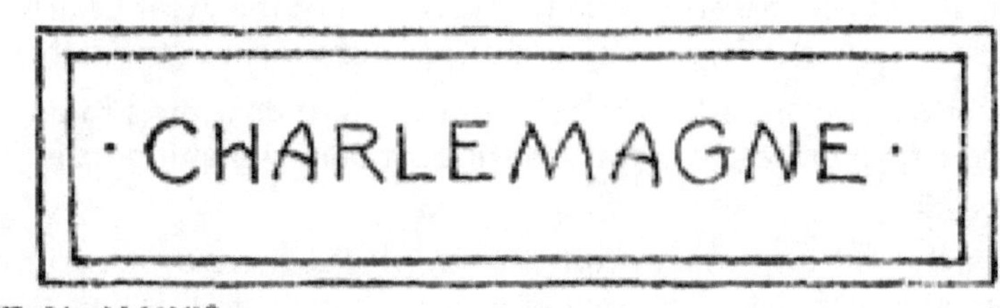

.B·McMANUS.

CHARLEMAGNE

With hasty fingers he seized the token, and, as he removed it, a loud wail startled the silence of the death-chamber and aroused the king. *The spell was broken.*

Throwing but a single glance at the corpse of his wife, Charlemagne left the chamber, and, even as he went, agreed to the archbishop's arrangements for her burial.

The grave so secretly made ready was unnecessary, however, for the body was borne to Mayence, where a tomb raised to the memory of Frastrade is still to be seen.

At the archbishop's desire Charlemagne once more took his seat in the Council of State, and once more the Empire was put in order.

The courtiers resented the advent of the churchman into the favour of the Emperor, who at length, when the court was sitting at Aix-la-Chapelle, determined to rid himself of the mystic jewel. Choosing a dark night, he sought a deep pool near the centre of a morass as being suitable for concealing the gem, which he had determined no man should ever see. Coming upon the spot, and holding the bauble in his hand above the waters, he dropped it and saw it sink, as though the pit were bottomless. But the brilliancy of the gem was inextinguishable.

Next morning the court was pleased to note that the archbishop's influence over the Emperor was quite gone.

As the Emperor was strolling about the city, he fell upon the pool which held the gem. There he would sit by the hour, gazing upon the still waters, near which he afterward built himself a home, known to-day, though in ruins, as the castle of Frankenberg.

A few years after the death of his wife, Charlemagne built *La Chapelle*, that great octagonal church which gives the city its French name. The tomb of Charlemagne is there, inscribed only *Carolo Magno*. He died at Aix-la-Chapelle in 814, and was buried with great pomp. Victor Hugo gives Aix-la-Chapelle as the place of his birth, which is manifestly an error.

Charlemagne's body was placed in the tomb in a sitting posture, and three centuries later was exhumed by Frederick Barbarossa that he might sit in the same place, and afterward the German Emperors used the seat as a sort of throne of state at their coronations.

The sword and sceptre and all that was mortal of the great Charlemagne are gone, but his memory still lives in an enduring monument in the cathedral.

The cathedral is wonderful for its antiquary and charming to all who come within its spell; furthermore it forms a shrine for hero-worshippers which should not be neglected.

At one of the entrances is a bronze wolf, placed there to keep in memory a monkish legend which passes current at Aix-la-Chapelle to this day.

It runs as follows:

"In former times the zealous and devout inhabitants of Aix-la-Chapelle determined to build a cathedral. For six months the clang of the hammer and axe resounded with wonderful activity, but alas! the money which had been supplied by pious Christians for this holy work became exhausted, the wages of the masons were suspended, and with them their desire to hew and hammer, for, after all, men were not so very religious in those days as to build a temple on credit.

AIX-LA-CHAPELLE CATHEDRAL IN IXTH CENTURY

"Thus it stood, half-finished, resembling a falling ruin. Moss, grass, and wild parsley flourished in the cracks of the walls, screech-owls already discovered convenient places for their nests, and amorous sparrows hopped lovingly about where holy priests should have been teaching lessons of chastity.

"The builders were confounded; they endeavoured to borrow here and there, but no rich man could be induced to advance so large a sum. The collection from house to house fell short. When the magistracy received this report, they were out of humour, and looked with desponding countenances toward the cathedral walls, as fathers look upon the remains of favourite children.

"At this moment a stranger of commanding figure and something of pride in his voice and bearing entered and exclaimed: '*Bon Dieu!* they say that you are out of spirits. Hem! if nothing but money is wanting, you may console yourselves, gentlemen. I possess mines of gold and silver, and both can and will most willingly supply you with a ton of it.'

"The astounded Senators sat like a row of pillars, measuring the stranger from head to foot. The burgomaster first found his tongue. 'Who are you, noble lord,' said he, 'that thus, entirely unknown, speak of tons of gold as though they were sacks of beans? Tell us your name, your rank in this world, and whether you are sent from the regions above to assist us.'

"'I have not the honour to reside there,' replied the stranger, 'and, between ourselves, I beg most particularly to be no longer troubled with questions concerning who and what I am. Suffice it to say I have gold plentiful as summer hay!' Then, drawing forth a leathern pouch, he proceeded: 'This little purse contains the tenth of what I'll give. The rest shall soon be forthcoming. Now listen, my masters,' continued he, clinking the coin, 'all this trumpery is and shall remain yours if you promise to give me the first little soul that enters the door of the new temple when it is consecrated.'

"The astonished Senators now sprang from their seats as if they had been shot up by an earthquake, and then rushed pell-mell, and fell all of a lump into the farthest corner of the room, where they rolled and clung to each other like lambs frightened at flashes of lightning. Only one of the party, who had not entirely lost his wits, collected his remaining senses, and, drawing his head out of the heap, uttered boldly, 'Avaunt, thou wicked spirit!'

"But the stranger, who was no less a person than Master Urian, laughed at them. 'What's all this outcry about?' said he at length; 'is my offence so heinous that you are all become like children? It is I that may suffer from this business, not you. With my hundreds and thousands I have not far to run to buy a score of souls. From you I ask but one in exchange for all my money. What are you picking at straws for? One may plainly see you are a mere set of humbugs! For the good of the commonwealth (which high-sounding name is often borrowed for all sorts of purposes), many a prince would instantly conduct a whole army to be butchered, and you refuse one single man for that purpose! Fie! I am ashamed, O overwise counsellors, to hear you reason thus absurdly and citizen-like. What! do you think to deprive yourselves of the kernel of your people by granting my wish? Oh, no, there your wisdom is quite at fault, for, depend on it, hypocrites are always the earliest church-birds.'

"By degrees, as the cunning fiend thus spoke, the Senators took courage and whispered in each other's ear: 'What is the use of our resisting? The grim lion will only show his teeth once; if we don't assent, we shall infallibly be packed off ourselves. It is better, therefore, to quiet him directly.'

"Scarcely was this sanguinary contract concluded when a swarm of purses flew into the room through the doors and windows, and Urian, more civil than before, took leave without leaving any smell behind. He stopped, however, at the door, and called out with a grim leer: 'Count it over again, for fear that I may have cheated you.'

"The hellish gold was piously expended in finishing the cathedral, but, nevertheless, when the building shone forth in all its splendour, the whole town was filled with fear and alarm at the sight of it. The fact was that, although the Senators had promised by bond and oath not to trust the secret to anybody, one of them had prated to his wife, and she had made it a market-place tale, so that all declared they would never set foot within the temple. The terrified council now consulted the clergy, but the good priests all hung down their heads. At last a monk cried out: 'A thought strikes me. The wolf which has so long ravaged the neighbourhood of our town was this morning caught alive. This will be a well-merited punishment for the destroyer of our flocks; let him be cast to the devil in the fiery gulf. 'Tis possible the arch hell-hound may not relish this breakfast, yet *nolens volens* he must swallow it. You promised him certainly a soul, but whose was not decidedly specified.'

"The monk's plan was plausible, and the Senate determined to put the cunning trick into execution. At length the day of consecration arrived, and orders were given to bring the wolf to the principal entrance of the cathedral. So, just as the bells began to ring, the trap-door of the cage was pulled open, and the savage beast darted out into the nave of the empty church. Master Urian, from his lurking-place, beheld this consecration offering with the utmost fury. Burning with choler at being thus deceived, he raged like a tempest and then rushed forth, slamming the brass gate so violently after him that the rings split in two.

"This crack, which serves to commemorate the priest's victory over the tricks of the devil, is still exhibited to the gaping travellers who visit the cathedral."

So much for the legend. But the devil, disappointed at the turn of affairs in respect to the cathedral, had his revenge when Aix, fifty years or more ago, first became the centre of public gaming-tables, which only lately have been deserted by what is known as smart society for other resorts of a similar nature elsewhere.

There can be no question but that Charlemagne's church at Aix, while it is itself a rather vivid memory of Ravenna, is the prototype of much church-building elsewhere. The round churches of Germany followed in due course, while, in respect to some details, the cathedral has been claimed to be the forerunner of the true Gothic. At any rate, there is a reflection of its dome in that which terminates the centre of the cross of St. Fédêle at Como. The similarity goes to prove that Charlemagne's industry in church-building in Italy was as great as his desire of conquest.

The church at Aix-la-Chapelle was frankly designed as the tomb of Charlemagne, and that perhaps accounts for the combining of the rotunda of a ceremonial edifice with that of a basilica intended solely for worship. Part of it was undoubtedly the work of the Comacine builders whom Charlemagne brought from Italy, and part is nothing more than an importation or adaptation of classical and Byzantine adornments.

AIX-LA-CHAPELLE CATHEDRAL

Charlemagne's architects studied geography and climate well when they erected this link between the Romanesque-Lombardic style of the south and the Gothic of the north.

That portion of the present cathedral at Aix-la-Chapelle which was built by Charlemagne is the octagonal projection toward the east. It forms a truly regal mausoleum, and for twelve hundred years has well stood the march of time.

It is supposed to have been the most magnificent church edifice of Charlemagne's era throughout all Europe, though it was seriously injured by an earthquake a few years after its completion.

Later it was plundered by the Normans, and it suffered disastrous fires in 1146, 1234, 1236, and 1656, having in consequence undergone many material changes.

Its external features have been considerably added to, but the prototype of the round and octagonal churches, subsequently erected in Germany, is here visible to-day in all its comparative novelty.

The granite and porphyry columns which support the arches giving upon the interior of the octagon were once taken and carried to Paris, but fortunately they were returned and again put into position.

The choir of the church, as it now is, was not begun until 1353, and was finished in the century following. It is pure Gothic of the most approved variety, whereas the octagon church is as pure Romanesque; and the two components do not blend or mingle in the least.

In the roof of the octagon is a remarkable specimen of modern wall and roof decoration, which might better have been omitted.

There is a cloister leading from the northwest chapel which has recently been restored. It is a delightful retreat, and has the "stations of the cross" displayed upon its inner wall.

There are numerous rare and valuable relics in the cathedral; the chief of which is the flagstone, which, bearing the simple words, *Carolo Magno*, is supposed to cover the actual burial-place of Charlemagne. Above this is a magnificent chandelier, reminiscent of another in the church at Hildesheim, the gift of the Emperor Frederick Barbarossa.

Eight chapels surround the octagon, and in the Chapel of the Holy Cross is a magnificent altar-piece consisting of a crucifix carved in wood.

Most of the kings and queens who were crowned at Aix-la-Chapelle presented articles of value to the sacristy. The most magnificent of these is a sarcophagus in Parian marble representing the Rape of Proserpine.

The marble chair on which Charlemagne was found sitting in his tomb, and upon which the German emperors were crowned, is yet to be seen.

The relics in the cathedral are divided into two classes. In the first class are those which are the most sacred; in the second class are those of lesser importance. The latter are visible at all times; the former only once in seven years, when they are exposed for a fortnight.

The choir-stalls are set against the walls in a curious fashion, and there are chairs instead of the usual German benches for the congregation.

The appearance of this celebrated cathedral from the outside is most curious, since the erections and additions of later centuries have not been symmetrical.

There is a tall, modern spire which is not a beautiful addition, and the magnificent octagon has had a slate roof added, which likewise is a detraction.

St. Adelbert's was another ancient church of Aix-la-Chapelle, but it has given way to a modern edifice bearing the same name, though it is in good taste and most pleasing in its interior arrangement.

The Minoriten Kirche is a monkish foundation of the fourteenth or fifteenth century. Its nave and aisles all come under one canopy vault, and its aisleless choir is squared off abruptly with an enormous carved and painted altar-piece of no great excellence.

It is pleasant to recall here that the council of Aix-la-Chapelle made laws, which Charlemagne himself encouraged, referring to the treatment of pilgrims by the hospices which were so generally established throughout Charlemagne's realm in Carlovingian times.

To the ordinary fine for murder there was added sixty *soldi* more if the person killed were a pilgrim to or from a hospice. Any who denied food and shelter to a pilgrim was fined three *soldi*. These were the regulations put into effect through Charlemagne's dominions at the suggestion of Pepin II.

COAT OF ARMS, AIX-LA-CHAPELLE

CHAPTER XXVIII
LIÈGE

The natural highway from Antwerp and Brussels to the Rhine lies through Liège and Aix-la-Chapelle, or Aachen, as the Germans call the latter.

Wordsworth, in his wonderful travel poem, wrote of the Meuse, which flows by Liège on its way to the Royal Ardennes, in a way which should induce many sated travellers to follow in his footsteps, and know something of the fascinating charm of this most fertile and perhaps the most picturesque of all the rivers of Europe.

> "What lovelier home could gentle fancy choose?
> In this the stream, whose cities, heights and plains,
> War's favourite playground, are with crimson stains
> Familiar, as the morn with pearly dews.

* * * * * * * * * *

> "How sweet the prospect of yon watery glade,
> With its gray locks clustering in pensive shade,
> That, shap'd like old monastic turrets, rise,
> From the smooth meadow ground serene and still."

As one journeys on to Liège, Roman influences have left many and visible remains.

Crossing the plain of Neervinden, one enters the province of the Liègeois, where the French were defeated by the Austrians in 1793, thus releasing Belgium from the Gallic yoke.

At Landen one recalls that it is the town of the inception of the family of Charlemagne which gave to France her second race of kings.

Liège has been called the Birmingham of Continental Europe. It might better be called one of the foremost industrial centres of the world, for such it is to-day.

It is beautifully placed in an amphitheatre-like valley, and its tall chimneys, its smoke, and its grind of wheels bespeak an activity and unrest of which the former ages knew not.

Formerly the Liègeois were a turbulent and truculent folk, if one is to believe history.

If, however, one does not care to go back to history, he might turn to the pages of "Quentin Durward" and read of the spirit of romance which once surrounded Liège and its people.

GENERAL VIEW OF LIÈGE

The famous "Legend of the Liègeois" recounts how a working blacksmith found an inexhaustible supply of coals for his forge through the aid of a gnomish old man.

Previously the smith's fires had burned low, and only the old man's song inspired him to forage on the hillside, with the result that the future prosperity of the city grew up from the accessibility of this inexhaustible coal supply.

The old man's story ran thus:

> "Wine's good in wintry weather.
> Up the hillside near the heather,
> Go and gather the black earth,
> It shall give your fire birth.
> Ill fares the hide when the buckler wants mending,
> Ill fares the plough when the coulter wants tending."

When Liège, through its prosperity, had grown to good proportions, its government was assigned to a sort of prelate-proprietor.

These princely prelates were often but lads of eighteen or twenty, who became identified with the Church, frequently enough, simply because of the power it gave them.

The craftsmen and artisans of the city bought many rights from time to time from the bishops, and finally wrested the power from out of the hands of the Church, much as did the burghers of other cities from their feudal lords.

Then followed the struggle, which in Flanders raged perhaps more bitterly than elsewhere in Europe; the rising, where the many fought against the privileged few, and much riot and bloodshed was caused on all sides.

Then came first the burgher heroes of Liège, who, like their confrères in Ghent and Bruges, found in many instances the martyrdom of the patriot.

In the Place St. Lambert formerly stood—until 1801, when it was removed after having been damaged by a mob—the former cathedral of St. Lambert, which took its name from the first bishop of Liège. This ancient cathedral was of much grandeur and magnificence, attributes which the present cathedral of St. Paul decidedly lacks.

It was in this venerable cathedral of St. Lambert that Quentin Durward went to hear mass, as we learn from Scott's novel, and here also, after the famous siege of Liège by Louis XI. and Charles the Bold, the two princes themselves repaired for the same purpose. St. Lambert of Liège and the three Kings of Cologne were, it would appear, the chief patrons to whom Quentin and his early followers made their vows.

The bishopric was founded by Héraclius in 968, and a church, of which the present choir is a part, was built upon the site of the present St. Paul's in the thirteenth century. The see was formerly a suffragan of Cologne, and the only bishopric in the Low Countries except Tournai and Utrecht.

The present cathedral is consistently enough a Gothic church, but it is not a satisfactory example, in spite of its magnificent proportions.

Of a cruciform plan, and with a nave which was only completed in 1528, it is a poor apology for a great Gothic church, such as we know at Metz, Nancy, or even at Brussels.

Its western tower, satisfactory enough in itself, is crowned with a ludicrous spire, which dates only from 1812.

Since St. Lambert's has disappeared, and the present St. Paul's dates only from the ante-Revolutionary days, the chief ecclesiastical treasure of the city is the Église St. Jacques. It was founded in 1014 by the Bishop Baudry II., but the Romanesque tower to the west is of the century following, and the whole fabric was very much modified in 1513-38.

It is a magnificent flamboyant Gothic church of quite the first rank, when compared with others of its kind elsewhere.

It has an ample nave and aisles with a polygonal choir and a series of radiating chapels which are singularly beautiful.

The magnificent north portal is an addition of the sixteenth century.

The interior has been called Spanish in its motive. Certainly it is not quite like any other Gothic forms we know in these parts, and does bear some resemblance to that peculiar variety of Gothic which belongs to Spain.

The choir has some fine glass showing the armorial bearings of former patrons of the church.

There is a beautiful carved stone staircase and much sculptured stonework in the choir.

The organ-buffet is ornate, even of its kind,—a masterpiece of cabinet-making,—and was the work of Andre Severin of Maestricht in 1673.

The left transept, which is some thirty feet longer than the right, has a fine painting of a "Mater Dolorosa," while, opposite, is a stone monument to the founder of the church, Baudry II., of Renaissance workmanship.

St. Jean is another pre-tenth-century foundation of the Bishop Notger, somewhat after the plan of the "round church" at Aix-la-Chapelle. It was entirely rebuilt, however, in the eighteenth century, though the original octagon was kept intact.

At some distance from the city, on a height which may be truly called dominating, is the church of St. Martin, founded in 962, and reconstructed, after the Gothic manner of the time, contemporary with St. Jacques. Of recent times it has been restored. If any separation or division of its parts can be made, one concludes that the choir is German, and its nave French.

In 1246 there was held in this church a *Fête Dieu* following upon a vision of Ste. Julienne, the abbess of Cornillon near Liège. The fête was ordained by Pope Urban IV., who himself had been a canon of the cathedral of Liège.

Ste. Croix was another of Notger's foundations, in 979, on the site of an ancient château.

The choir was built toward 1175, and has an octagonal tower with a gallery of small columns just under the roof, after the manner known as distinctly Rhenish.

The church exhibits thoroughly that Rhine manner of building which made combined use of the Gothic and Romanesque,—in bewildering fashion, to one who has previously known only the comparatively pure types of France.

The nave and its aisles rise to the same height, but the apsidal choir is aisleless.

The general effect of the interior is light and graceful, with circular columns in a blue-gray stone, which is very beautiful.

A series of fourteenth or fifteenth century "Stations of the Cross" fill the arches of the transepts; quite an unusual arrangement of this feature, and one which seems well considered.

St. Barthélemy's is Liège's other great church. It is a *basilica* of five naves and two Romanesque towers. It dates in reality from the twelfth century, but has been greatly modernized.

St. Barthélemy's might have been a highly interesting example of a Romanesque church had it not been desecrated by late Italian details.

St. Barthélemy's has a twelfth-century art treasure in a brazen font, cast in 1112 by Patras, a brass-founder of Dinant on the Meuse. Its bowl depicts five baptismal scenes in high relief, each accompanied by a descriptive legend. Upon the rim of the bowl is the following legend:

> *"Bissenis bobus pastorum forma notatur,*
> *Quos et apostolice commendat gratia vite,*
> *Officiiq; gradus quo fluminis impetus bujus*
> *Letificat sanctam purgatis civibus urbem."*

COAT OF ARMS, LIÈGE

CHAPTER XXIX
DÜSSELDORF, NEUSS,
AND MÜNCHEN-GLADBACH

Düsseldorf

AMONG æsthetic people in general, Düsseldorf is revered—or was revered, though the time has long since passed—for that style of pictorial art known to the world as the Düsseldorf School.

A remarkably good collection of pictures remains in its art gallery to remind us of the fame of Düsseldorf as an art centre, but to-day its art has become "old-fashioned," and the gay little metropolis has many, if more worldly, counter attractions.

Düsseldorf takes its name from the little river Düssel which joins the Rhine at this point.

The French guide-books call Düsseldorf the *"plus coquettes des bords du Rhin"*; and so it really is, for few tourists go there for its churches alone, though they are by no means squalid or inferior.

The city was the residence of the Counts, afterward the Dukes, of Berg—for it was made a duchy by the Emperor Wenceslaus—from the end of the thirteenth century to the beginning of the nineteenth.

In 1806 Napoleon made it the capital of a new Grand Duchy of Berg in favour of Joachim Murat. By the treaty of 1815 Düsseldorf fell to Prussia, and became the chief town of the regency of Düsseldorf, and the seat of a superior court of justice.

Occupying the site that it does, on the banks of a great waterway, the city naturally became the centre of an important commerce.

Düsseldorf is the birthplace of many who have borne great names; of the philosopher Jacobi and his poet brother; the Baron de Hompesch, the last grand master of the Order of Malta; Von Ense, the eminent litterateur; the poet Heinrich Heine (who died at Paris in 1855), and the painters Cornelius, Lenzen, and Achenbach.

The principal church edifice is that dedicated to St. Lambert, the Hofkirche. It has a strong and hardy tower, very tall, and surmounted by a slate-covered spire. The ogival style predominates, and the fabric dates mostly from the fourteenth century. Its chief feature is its choir, which is far more ample and beautiful than the nave. The rest of the edifice fails to express any very high ideals of church-building.

At the foot of the apside, behind the choir, is a mausoleum erected in the seventeenth century for the elector, John Wilhelm, who died in 1690.

In the ambulatory of the choir is, on the left, a florid Gothic tabernacle, and by the second pillar of the nave is a colossal statue of St. Christopher. There are many tombs of Jacobeans, and of the Dukes of Berg.

There are also a number of paintings by Düsseldorf artists scattered about the church, but they have not the qualities exhibited by the old Flemish masters, and are hardly worthy of remark.

On the exterior of the southern wall is affixed an immense Calvary, which is theatrical in the extreme, and is not dignified nor churchly.

The Jesuit church is not remarkable architecturally, but there are a number of tombs therein of the princes of the house of Neubourg.

The ruins of the ancient château of Düsseldorf suggest but faintly its former glories before it was destroyed by the French bombardment of the city in the eighteenth century.

It has been restored, in a way, but with little regard for historical traditions, and a part of the edifice was made the home of the famous Düsseldorf academy of painting, founded in 1777 by Charles Theodore and reëstablished in 1822. It gave birth to a celebrated school of painting, now all but dead. Among the famous and well-known names connected therewith are: Cornelius, Schadow, Lessing, Schirmer, Hildebrand, and Koehler; the American, Lentzen; the Norwegians, Tiédemann and Gude; the landscape painters, Weber and Fay; and the historical painters, Knaus, Hübner, and Scheuren; and finally the celebrated engraver, Keller.

The museum and the gallery of paintings are still superb, and form a contribution to the history of the art of all ages which would be quite incomplete without it.

There are ten churches in Düsseldorf, and a synagogue, but in truth there is not much of interest in them all, and the "handsomest city of Germany" must rest its fame on something more than its appeal to the lover of churches.

Neuss

There is not much about the compact, though rather ungainly, little city of Neuss to interest any but the lover of churches, though its history is very ancient, and the development of its patronymic through *Novesium, Niusa,* and *Nova Castra* bespeaks volumes for the part it has played in the past.

Its origin dates back to the time of Drusus, and it is mentioned by Tacitus as the winter quarters of the Roman Army. The city was ravaged by Attila in 451, and by the Normans in the ninth century. Emperor Philip of Suabia captured it in 1206, and gave it to the Archbishop of Cologne. A chapter of nobles was founded here in 825, and Count Evrard of Clèves and Bertha, his wife, erected, in the first years of the thirteenth century, its principal church dedicated to St. Quirinus.

This church stands to-day, with its great square tower looming bulkily over the house-tops, and is reckoned as the prototype of many similar structures else-where. It has the almost perfect disposition and development of the double apse so frequently met with in German churches.

In general, its architecture is of a heavy order, and the whole structure is grim, though by no means gaunt nor cold.

NEUSS CATHEDRAL

St. Quirinus is of the epoch when the Romanesque was being replaced nearly everywhere by the new-coming Gothic.

In spite of this, its style is, curiously enough, neither one nor the other, nor is it transition, though the pointed arch has crept in and often eliminated the Romanesque attributes of the round-arch style round about. It is manifestly not transition, because there was no transition here from Romanesque to Gothic. It remained palpably Romanesque in spite of Gothic interpolations.

In the windows one can but remark the indecision which prompted the builders to fashion them in such extraordinary squat shapes, and they certainly serve their purpose of lighting the interior very badly.

The nave and aisles of St. Quirinus are ample, and its spacious *männerchöre* in the triforium is like all its fellows in the German churches, an adjunct which adds to the general effect of size.

The church dates from 1209, the period when the Gothic influence was not only making itself felt over the border, in the domain of France and Burgundy, but was already extending its influence elsewhere. But here, westward even of the borders of the Rhine, the round arch lingered on, to the exclusion of any very marked Gothic tendency.

There is an inscription in stone on the south wall of the church which places the date of its erection beyond all doubt. It reads thus:

ANNO . INCARNA.
DNI . MC.C.V.I.I.I.
PMO . IPERII . AN
NO . OTTONIS . A
DOLFO . COLON

EPO . SOPHIA . A
BBA . MAGISTER
WOLBERO . PO
SUIT . PMU . LAP

IDE . FUNDAME
NTI . HUI . TEM
PLI . I . DIE . SCI . DI
ONISII . MAR.

When a former Count of Clèves founded the primitive church here in the ninth century, it was a collegiate church attached to the abbey of which the mother superior was the Abbess Sophia, presumably the same referred to in the above inscription. The abbey itself was destroyed in 1199 during a civil warfare.

Though not really a massive structure, the church of St. Quirinus is, in every particular, of a strength and solidity which rank it as a masterwork of its age. There is nothing weak and attenuated about it, and its transepts and apses make up in general effect what it lacks in actual area.

The façade is imposing, though decidedly bizarre when compared with the simple flowing lines of Gothic; but, on the whole, the effect is one of a certain grandeur.

The aisles are astonishingly tall when compared with the nave.

There are various meetings of round-arched windows and arcades with those of a pointed nature, but there is not the slightest evidence of a development or transition from one to the other, hence the Gothic strain may be said not to exist.

The general effect of the exterior is polychromatic, which is not according to the best conceptions of ecclesiastical decorations in architecture. A twilight or a moonlight view, however, tones it all down in a manner that makes the fabric appear quite the most imposing church of its size that one may find in these parts.

The great central tower, reminiscent enough of the parish church in England, but not so frequent in Germany, and still less so in France, forms a great lantern which rises over the crossing in a marvellous and exceedingly practical manner, in that it affords about the only adequate means of admitting light into the interior.

The triforium of the nave is the chief interior feature to be remarked, and is most spaciously planned. It forms the *männerchöre* before mentioned.

The clerestory windows are decidedly Rhenish in character, resembling, says one antiquary, who is a humourist if nothing else, an ace of clubs. At any rate, it is a most unusual and inefficient manner of lighting a great church. These windows are practically trefoils of most unsymmetrical proportions, and are in every way unlovely.

The choir is raised on a platform, beneath which is the crypt. Three flights of steps lead to this platform, which gives it a far more grand appearance than its actual dimensions would otherwise allow.

The choir-stalls are of the fourteenth century, and are the only mediæval furnishings to be seen in the church to-day.

The apses contain only moderately effective glass.

The frescoes in the cupola of St. Quirinus, which are the work of Cornelius of Düsseldorf (about 1811), are most interesting, and are among the most successful of the great number of modern works of their kind to be seen in Germany.

München-Gladbach

München-Gladbach is one of those "snug" little German towns that one comes across now and then when wandering along off the beaten track. Its streets are trim and clean, and its houses likewise, with a brilliancy of fresh paint which is consistently and proverbially Dutch. Beneath one's foot is a sea of cobblestones all worn to a smoothness which argues the tramp of countless hordes of feet over centuries of time, if paving-stones have really been invented so long. With all its air of prosperity and providence, München-Gladbach is not a highly interesting town in which to linger.

Its name is compounded of its prefix, meaning *monk's*, with its original patronymic, Gladbach. The monks of Gladbach were a part of the establishment which founded the minster church of Gladbach, an old abbey or monastic edifice which stands to-day, a great transeptless thirteenth-century structure with an elevated choir reached from the nave by two flights of ten or a dozen steps.

The crypt is entered from between these two flights of steps, and forms all that is left to mark the primitive church.

The round-arched style and Gothic, of a sort, intermingle in the nave in bewildering fashion until one wonders in what classification it really belongs. The openings from the aisles to the nave are pointed, while above is an unpierced triforium with a clerestory of round-headed arches.

In the aisles are what Jacobean architects called fanlights, a series of peculiarly shaped openings like an oddly shaped fan. They are distinctly Rhenish; indeed they are not acknowledged to be found elsewhere, and hence may be considered as one of the chief points of distinction of this otherwise not remarkably appealing church.

There are no aisles in the choir, which dates from the thirteenth century and terminates with a multi-sided apse pierced by long lancet windows.

The Stadt Kirche of Gladbach, or the parish church as it properly takes rank, is still a Catholic edifice and shows the advantage of having been kept in active use. There is nothing musty or moss-grown about it, but in every way it is as warmly appealing as the monks' church is coldly unattractive.

There is no marked choir termination, its great aisles extending completely to the rear with just a suspicion of a rudimentary pentagonal apse to suggest the easterly end. This is a common enough arrangement in German churches, which more frequently than not, in the fourteenth century, the date of this structure, possessed nothing but a squared-off east end, after the English manner of building.

At the westerly end is a well-planned tower distinctly Rhenish—if it were not it would be thought heavy—and where the choir is supposed to join the nave the roof is surmounted by a tiny spire, which, in truth, is no addition of beauty.

The interior shows great height, and, if of no great architectural splendour, has enough mural embellishment and attractive glass to stamp it as a livable and lovable edifice for religious worship, which is a good deal more than most modern church buildings ever acquire.

The six bays of the nave show pointed arches springing from rounded columns. There is an arcaded triforium, and an elaborate series of clerestory windows which show the geometrical and flamboyant Gothic in its perfection.

The apse is lighted with five windows of great height. The glass is a mixture of colour and monotone, but the effect is undeniably good.

The chancel is so shallow that the choir flows over, as it were, into one bay of the nave, while the choir-stalls themselves are placed in the aisles. Certainly a most unusual, and perhaps a unique, arrangement.

An altar fronts the west end of either range of stalls, and back, at the easterly end of the aisles, is found another altar.

The high altar has a handsome modern screen in the form of a gilt triptych, which is singularly effective and imposing.

Beneath the tower, at the westerly end, is the baptistery, entrance to which from the body of the church is gained through a low, pointed arch.

COAT OF ARMS, DÜSSELDORF

CHAPTER XXX
ESSEN AND DORTMUND

Essen

LYING just to the eastward of the Rhine are Essen and Dortmund.

The former was once the site of a powerful abbey of Benedictine nuns, which was dissolved in 1803. The abbess of Essen was always a titled person, and was a member of the Westphalian circle of the Imperial Estates, in which capacity she held a governing right over a large tract of country immediately surrounding the abbey.

There are the spires of five churches hidden away in the forest of chimneys of the manufactories of Essen which rise skyward from the Rhineland plain. It is not a very beautiful picture that one sees from across the railway viaduct, but a remarkable one, and one that has undeniable elements of the picturesque.

The cathedral at Essen is a conglomerate group of buildings of many epochs. The church proper consists of a three-aisled nave, with the usual choir appendage in what must pass for acceptable Gothic.

There are Romanesque features which date back as far as 874, when the original edifice was built by Bishop Alfred of Hildesheim. The crypt, the transept, and possibly a part of the choir foundation, are of the eleventh century, and are of Romanesque motive; but the Gothic fabric superimposes itself upon these early works in the style in vogue in the fourteenth century.

There are evidences of a central octagon, like that at Aix-la-Chapelle, and St. Géréon's at Cologne, but the fourteenth-century rebuilding has practically covered this up, though three of the original faces are left, and bear aloft a series of tall Corinthian columns.

The nave, for some reason, inexplicable on first sight, is low and unimpressive, caused doubtless by the grandeur of the supporting pillars of the roof and the shallowness of the groining above.

The pillars are single cylinders with curiously plain capitals.

The choir rises a few steps above the nave pavement, in order to give height to the crypt ambulatory, as is frequently the custom in German churches.

The windows of the south aisle are good in their design and glass, which, though modern, reflects the Gothic mediæval spirit far better than is usual.

GENERAL VIEW OF ESSEN

There is an elevated gallery along the aisle walls, which forms a sort of tribune or *männerchöre*. In one of the recesses beneath the gallery is a highly coloured sculpture group of an "Entombment."

The easterly portion of the cathedral is by far the most pleasing, and partakes of the best Gothic features, and indeed is far superior to the nave. The supporting columns of the vaulting have foliaged capitals, while the vaulting itself is even more elaborate.

SEVEN-BRANCHED CANDLESTICK, ESSEN

The aisles, as they approach the choir, are rectangular-ended, and extend quite to the end of the choir termination, showing a very singular cross-section of this portion of the church.

The screen is a modern stone work after the Gothic manner. It sits beneath a not unbeautiful Gothic window, rather richly traceried with four lights. The glass of this window is modern, but, like that in the nave aisles, is excellent.

The crypt is entered from the south transept, and also from the nave by an entrance which passes between the steps which rise to the choir pavement.

There is an elaborate seven-branched candlestick at the juncture of the nave and choir, modelled on one known to have existed in the Temple at Jerusalem. It is of the conventional form, but is a rare piece of church furniture in that it dates from 1003, when it was presented by the Abbess Matilda, sister of the Emperor Otho II. Since it stands six or eight feet in height, this candlestick is a notable and conspicuous object.

Before the steps leading to the crypt is the tomb of Bishop Alfred of Hildesheim. The crypt is all that a crypt should be,—a dim-lighted, solemn chamber of five aisles, the pavement of the church above being supported on stubby square pillars. It is used also for devotional purposes, the altar at the easterly end of the central aisle bearing the inscription, *"Heilige Maria, Trösterin der Betrubten, bitt fur uns."*

The cloisters of this interesting edifice are, in part, of the primitive style of early Gothic, while the southern and western sides are an approach to the full-blown Gothic of a later epoch, with foliaged capitals.

Dortmund

Dortmund is the largest town of the province of Westphalia, and possesses four mediæval churches of more than usual interest.

St. Reinhold's is the chief, and is a cruciform edifice of more than ordinary proportions. It is a picturesque mélange of many parts. Its western tower is of no style in particular, and is hideous, but most curious considering its environment. The nave and transepts are supposedly of the thirteenth century, but they are certainly not good Gothic as we know it elsewhere.

The choir is of the early fifteenth century, and is much more gracefully conceived than is any other portion of this nondescript edifice.

The transepts are square boxlike protuberances, which link the choir with the nave in most unappealing fashion.

In the interior the most astonishing features are the low truncated nave of three bays, the grimness of the walls of the entire fabric,—excepting the well-lighted and aspiring choir,—and the straight-backed pews.

The clerestory windows of the nave are semicircular, but the aisles are lighted by Gothic openings.

There are two altars, one at the choir entrance and the other in the apse, each surmounted by a triptych.

The windows of the choir-apse, tall, ample, and of admirable framing, are the chief glory of this not very beautiful, though interesting, church.

St. Mary's is a late twelfth-century Romanesque structure, without transepts, but possessed of a towering apsidal choir.

The nave is an attenuated affair with no triforium, leaving a vast blank wall space, as though it were intended to have been decorated.

Dortmund's "Pfarr Kirche" was a former Dominican foundation. Its general proportions are far greater than those of any other of the city's churches. The nave is ample, and the great choir of four bays, with spacious, lofty windows, is of the same generous proportions.

The church dates only from the mid-fourteenth century, and its three-bayed nave is even later. The aisles of the nave are curious in that they are not of similar dimensions. That on the street side is separated from the nave proper by square piers, with a slender shaft running to the vaulting. The other aisle is more ample, and has its arched openings to the nave composed of four shafts superimposed upon a central cylinder.

The nave lighting is amply provided for by a series of four light windows, bare, however, of any glass worthy of remark.

The south wall, which has no windows, has two large frescoes, a "Descent of the Holy Ghost" and an "Assumption." There is also a series of paintings by two native artists, Heinrich and Victor Dunwege.

COAT OF ARMS, ESSEN

CHAPTER XXXI
EMMERICH, CLÈVES, AND XANTEN

Emmerich and Clèves

JUST below Emmerich, which is the last of the German Rhenish cities, the Rhine divides itself, and, branching to the north, takes the Dutch name of Oud Rijn, which name, with the variation Neder Rijn, it retains until it reaches the sea. The branch to the west takes the name of the Waal and passes on through Nymegen, bounding Brabant on the north, and enters the sea beyond Dordrecht.

Emmerich has, in its church of St. Martin, a tenth-century church of no great architectural worth, but charming to contemplate, nevertheless.

Four kilometres away is Clèves, which, under the Romans, was known as Clivia and attained considerable prominence and prosperity. The Normans sacked it in the ninth century, but it was shortly rebuilt, and became the chief town of the County, afterward the Duchy, of Clèves.

Under the Empire the city belonged to France. The town's principal church is quite attractive, but, beyond the distinction which it has in its twin spires, terminating a singularly long line of roof-top of nave and choir, there are no architectural features of note.

Xanten

At a little distance from the Rhine, just before the frontier of Holland is reached, is Xanten, the ancient Ulpia Castra. Near by, in the neighbouring village of Mirten, one sees the remains of an ancient amphitheatre, which denotes a considerable importance for the neighbourhood in Roman times. If more proof were needed, it will be found in the museum at Bonn, where are many Roman antiquities coming from the neighbourhood.

Xanten is celebrated for having given birth to St. Norbert, the founder of the order of Premonstratension monks, and for having been the cradle of Siegfried, the hero of the "Nibelungen Lied."

The city was captured by the French in 1672.

The collegiate church of Xanten is known as St. Victor's, and is truly celebrated for the grace and beauty of its early twelfth-century Gothic.

Without transepts or clerestory, it shows in its one ample chamber, comprising both nave and choir, an exemplification of the art of combining the accessories of the Latin-cross structures of France with the hall-church idea so frequently met with in Germany, and so well recognized as a distinct German type.

ST. VICTOR'S, XANTEN

This arrangement does not give the church the appearance of being in any way confined or limited; quite the reverse is the case, and the double range of windows in the apse indicates, at least, a loftiness and hardiness of construction which is highly commendable.

There are, moreover, double aisles to both nave and choir which give an ampleness to the interior which even its abundance of furnishings does not overcrowd.

There are few five-aisled churches such as this in Germany, or indeed elsewhere, Cologne being Germany's chief example in this style.

In general, the Gothic of this highly interesting church is of the best, though it dates from various periods. The primitive church, we know, was a Romanesque structure; but, beyond the foundations of the western towers, and possibly other fragmentary works yet hidden, there is nothing but the most acceptable Gothic in evidence.

A distinctly curious feature is the apse-sided termination to the aisles, radiating from the main apse at an angle of forty-five degrees. It is a distinct innovation in the easterly termination of a church; a sort of a compromise between the French, English, and German styles, and wholly a successful one.

In the chancel is a sort of screen before the high altar, worked in brass at Maastricht in 1501.

The windows contain a great deal of beautiful old glass, and some other that is by no means as good.

The clerestory windows are elaborately traceried, and there is much detail of church furnishings, a choir screen, some elaborate stalls, a little tapestry,—which looks well and is certainly old,—and a modern tiled floor which is not offensive.

As is frequently seen in Germany, the pillars and shafts have a series of statues superimposed upon them; always a daring thing to do, but in this case of far better execution and design than is frequently encountered. Before the church is a monument in honour of Cornelius de Pauw, the friend of the great Frederick, a canon of the church and a famous spiritual writer. He was born at Amsterdam in 1739 and died at Xanten in 1799.

CHAPTER XXXII

ARNHEIM, UTRECHT, AND LEYDEN

Arnheim

THE Rhine in Holland is a mighty river. It divides itself into many branches, all of which make their way to the sea through that country which Butler in the "Hudibras" calls:

> "A land that draws fifty feet of water,
> In which men live as in the very hold of nature,
> And when the sea does in upon them break,
> And drowns a province, does but spring a leak."

The Rhine proper, the Oud Rijn and the Neder Rijn, enfolds three great ecclesiastical centres of other days, Arnheim, Utrecht, and Leyden.

Arnheim is the chief town of the Guelderland, and seats itself proudly on the banks of the Neder Rijn just above its juncture with the Yssel. Of its fifty-five thousand inhabitants, twenty-five thousand are Roman Catholics, which fact makes it one of the most strongly Catholic cities, if not the strongest, in the Netherlands.

Formerly the city was known as the Arenacum of the Romans, and served as the residence of the Dukes of the Guelderland up to 1538. In 1579 it gave adherence to the "Union of Utrecht," and in 1672 was taken by the French, when it became one of the principal fortresses of Holland. To-day the fortifications serve the purpose to which they are so frequently devoted in the cities and towns of Continental Europe, and form a fine series of promenades.

In 1813 the town was taken by the Prussians, but in spite of all this changing of hands, it remains to-day as distinctly Dutch as any of the Low Country cities and towns. Its houses are well built of brick and equally well kept, and its sidewalks are as cleanly and well cared for as the courtyard of a palace.

GENERAL VIEW OF ARNHEIM

To-day the aspect of Arnheim is that of a quaint though modern-looking Dutch city. It is a favourite place of residence for *"messieurs du sucre,"* — rich Hollanders and Orientals from the Dutch East Indies. Altogether the atmosphere of its streets and cafés is decidedly cosmopolitan and most interesting.

The Groote Kerk, built in 1452, rises from the market-place with a considerable purity of Gothic style. The church was formerly dedicated to St. Eusebe. Its tower is a landmark for miles around, and rises to a height approximating three hundred feet. It is built of brick and is square for the first two tiers, flanked with sustaining buttresses, then it tapers off into an octagon. It contains a fine set of chimes, so frequently an adjunct to the churches and municipal belfries of the Low Countries.

The interior presents a great ogival example of the best of fourteenth and fifteenth century church-building.

To-day, since the church belongs to the Protestants, much that stood for symbolism in the Roman Church is wanting, and the pulpit, which is an admirable work of art in itself, is placed in the middle of the choir surrounded by numerous tribunes, or seats in tiers, in quite a parliamentary and non-churchly fashion.

Behind the choir is a monument to Charles d'Egmont, Duke of Guelderland, who died in 1538, and whose tomb is at Utrecht. As a work of art this monument in the Groote Kerk at Arnheim is much more worthy than such monuments usually are.

The duke is represented clothed in armour and reclining between six lions, which hold aloft his escutcheon.

The pedestal is ornamented with bas-reliefs representing the Holy Family, the twelve apostles, St. Christopher, and two other saints. On a pillar at the left of the tomb is suspended, in a sort of wooden cage, another figure of the same prince. The effigy is of painted wood and is amazingly lifelike, though smacking decidedly of the figures in a waxworks exhibition.

The *chevet* of this great church is quite worthy of consideration, though by no means as amply endowed as the French variety by which one comes to judge all others.

Altogether, except for the poverty of deeply religious symbolism in the interior, of which it has doubtless been despoiled since the Catholic religion has waned in its power here, the church is a lovely and lovable example of the appealing church edifices which one now and then comes across in Continental cities of the third rank.

The Catholic cult occupy the church of St. Walburge, a Gothic edifice in brick of the fourteenth century. At the portal are two great symmetrical towers which are worthy of a far more important edifice.

The interior is entirely modern as to its furnishings and fitments.

On four pillars of the nave are placed, back to back, statues of the evangelists, — a species of decorative embellishment which, at all times since the fifteenth century, has been greatly favoured throughout Germany and the Low Countries.

In France it is a feature but seldom seen, and, among the smaller parish churches, has almost its only examples at Vetheuil on the Seine below Paris, and at Louviers.

The high altar is modern, as are also the black and white marble baptismal fonts.

The pulpit is quite a grand affair, though modern also. Its sounding-board shows a figure of Moses holding aloft the tables of the law. It is admirably conceived and executed, and is of much artistic merit.

Arnheim possesses several other religious edifices; but, as satisfactory expressions of ecclesiastical art or architecture, they are quite unworthy. The only one worthy of remark—and that only for its unseemliness—is a modern Protestant place of worship in the form of a vast rotunda, which in all respects resembles a great building enclosing a panorama.

Behind the *chevet* of the Groote Kerk, the ancient cathedral, is a fine old-time house of the sixteenth century. It is known, somewhat sacrilegiously one thinks, as the Maison du Diable, and was formerly the residence of a famous brigand or highwayman,—if there be any subtle distinction between the two. This brigand was moreover of the nobility, and was known as Martens van Rosum, Duke of the Guelderland. In front of the house is a miniature terrace, and, on the walls above, to the right, are three monstrous effigies of devils, as well as one of a woman. In the centre, upon a pillar, is a bust of Van Rosum, and an inscription to the effect that the house was restored in 1830. To-day it is occupied by certain municipal offices.

Utrecht

In many respects Utrecht was, in the past, the most important city in Holland, not commercially, but politically.

To-day it is simply the capital of the province of Utrecht, the seat of a Catholic archbishop, and of a Jansenist archbishop as well.

Of its population of quite a hundred thousand souls, one-third, at least, are of the Catholic profession, which is an astonishing proportion for a city of Holland. For this reason, perhaps, the city remains the metropolis of the Catholic religion in the Netherlands.

The environs of the city are exceedingly picturesque. The Rhine again divides into two branches, the Oud Rijn continuing to the North Sea, through Leyden, and the other branch, known thenceforth as the Vecht, flowing into the Zuyder Zee.

Utrecht is one of the most ancient cities of the Netherlands, having been founded under Nero by a Roman Senator named Antony, hence it is frequently referred to by historians as Antonia Civitas.

Its name in time evolved itself into *Trajectum inferius* or *vetus,* and in the Latin nomenclature of the early middle ages, it became *Ultrajectum,* or *Trajectum Ultricensium.* Under the Franks it was called Wiltrecht, which was but a short step to the name it now bears.

King Dagobert here founded the first church in Friesland, with St. Willibrod as bishop, and St. Boniface, before he was called to Rome, here preached evangelization.

The city was ruined and devastated in the seventh century, but its rebuilding was begun in 718 by Clothaire IV. Toward 934 it was surrounded by protecting walls by Bishop Baldric of Clèves. Utrecht was frequently made the residence of the emperors, and Charles V. there built the château of Vreeburg, a species of fortress-château that was demolished by the burghers of the city at the beginning of the war of independence, 1577.

Adrien Florizoon, the preceptor of Charles V., who, at the death of Leo X., occupied the pontifical throne in 1522-23 as Adrien VI., was born at Utrecht. His house (Paushuizen) on the banks of the canal Nieuwe Gracht, now a government building, contains many pictures relative to his life and times.

For a long time the city was only a bishop's seat, but in 1559 it was made an archbishopric.

When, in 630, Dagobert, King of Austrasia, founded a chapel here, the religious foundation of the city began, and as early as in 696 it became the seat of a bishop. In the ninth century the Normans sacked the town, but thenceforth the bishops, who were then suffragans of Liège, acquired a strength and power which assured the city freedom from molestation for a long time.

In the sixteenth century political and religious dissension combined to promote a state of unrest which was most acute. In 1577 the party which had allied itself with the Prince of Orange introduced religious reform, and in 1579 the seven provinces of Holland formed their compact of federation, and the States General held their sittings here.

The *Domkerk*, or cathedral, originally dedicated to St. Martin, is to-day a Protestant church. It was an outgrowth of the primitive church founded in 630 by Dagobert I., and of an abbey established by St. Willibrod.

The cathedral of St. Martin was rebuilt, after a fire in 1024, by Bishop Adebolde, "in the presence of the Emperor Henry II. and many other great personages," as the old chroniclers have it. In 1257 it was nearly entirely rebuilt by the bishop then holding the see, Henri of Vianden, but a great storm crushed in its nave in 1674, since which time the faulty juncture of the various parts has been sadly apparent.

After the destruction of the nave, the choir and the transepts formed practically the entire building, with the tower existing merely as a dismembered and orphaned feature.

The tower was commenced in 1331 and completed in 1382. It rises from a magnificently vaulted base. The lower portion is rectangular, but the octagon which forms the upper stages and "pierced to the light of day," as the French have it, follows the best accepted style of its era. In its way it is, although quite different, the rival of St. Ouen's "Crown of Normandy" at Rouen.

There are 453 steps to be mounted if one cares to ascend to the platform, 103 metres from the ground. One gets the usual bird's-eye view, with this difference, that the glance of the eye seems to reach out into an interminable distance, by reason of the general flatness of the country. One sees, at any rate, quite all of the provinces of South Holland, with the Zuyder Zee to the north, and a part of Guelderland and North Brabant. The tower possesses also a fine set of chimes of forty-two bells which is reminiscent of Belgium; but, unlike those in the famous old belfry at Bruges, the chimes on the *Domkerk* at Utrecht do not ring out popular marches or the airs of popular songs.

GENERAL VIEW OF UTRECHT AND ITS CATHEDRAL

The interior is so crowded with benches, similar to what English churchgoing people know as pews, that its original aspect is somewhat changed. Eighteen great pillars hold aloft the vaulting of the choir and transepts.

A notable tomb in black and white marble is that of Admiral van Gent (1676), and another is that of Bishop Georges d'Egmont (1549). In the vault beneath the edifice were buried the viscera of Conrad II. and Henry V., who died at Utrecht, and whose remains, with this exception, were transported to Speyer.

A fine Gothic cloister connects the cathedral with the university. This has, in recent years, undergone restoration of a most practical and devoted kind. It is a marvel of modern architectural work.

St. Peter's is another ancient Roman Catholic church now devoted to Protestant uses.

St. John's also comes under this category. It is a fine example of a small Gothic church of the variety which was best known only in Holland and Belgium; much more severe than the French species, but interesting withal.

Within the walls of this last are two tombs quite worthy of attention and remark. The one against the western wall is that of a cardinal who died in the fifteenth century, and the other is that of Balthazar Frederick of Stoech. The latter, though dating only from the eighteenth century, is charmingly sculptured, and has two superb figures of weeping children done in marble.

The Roman Catholic church of St. Catherine is a Gothic edifice of the third ogival period, and was restored in 1880 at the expense of a devout Catholic of the city, named Van den Brink.

The walls are decorated in a polychromatic scheme, which is not beautiful, though undeniably striking. The jube, by Mengelberg of Utrecht, is distinctly good.

Utrecht possesses in the *Aartsbisschoppelyk Museum* an establishment unique among the museums of the world. Particularly it shows all branches of religious art, and is of great importance to all who study the art and architecture of the Netherlands.

Of the secular establishments one remarks the university which adjoins the cathedral. It dates from 1636, and has to-day five faculties.

In the palace, constructed for Louis Bonaparte during the Napoleonic overflow, is a magnificent library of 110,000 volumes and 1,500 MSS.

The ancient academy, the arch-episcopal palace, the Palais de Justice, the Stadt Huis, the Paushuizen (Prefecture), the mint, with a rich numismatic collection, and the Association of Arts and Sciences complete the list of the city's notable monuments.

Leyden

With Leyden the Rhine may be said to take its leave of ancient civilization, though it only joins the briny waters of the North Sea at Katwyck, a dozen kilometres distant, after having formed a natural frontier for nearly eleven hundred kilometres, from its Alpine cradle in the canton of Grisons.

Anciently Leyden was the Lugdunum Batavorum of the Romans, and, according to the old-time historians, was the most ancient city of Holland. Later its name became Leithen, from which its present nomenclature is evolved.

Its great importance came with the thirteenth century and endured until the Spanish wars.

The city was besieged by the Spaniards in 1574, and delivered therefrom by the Prince of Orange in the year following.

To-day the plan of Leyden forms a regular pentagon, with long streets and boulevards, all characteristically Dutch, with old-time and modern houses alike built with queer gabled roofs, giving quite a mediæval aspect to an otherwise lively and up-to-date little city.

The city is traversed from east to west by the Oud Rijn, which throws out many arms and branches and gives to the place a most Venetian appearance.

One distinctive feature of the topographical aspect of Leyden, and one which is universal in most of the cities of Holland, are the canals which cross and recross the principal streets. All is *plus propres*, as the French have it, and the tree-bordered, cobblestoned quays are not the least of the town's attractions for the stranger.

Unquestionably the chief architectural treasure of Leyden is the Stadt Huis. It is of the style which may best be called Dutch, and is a reconstruction of 1597.

In front of the Stadt Huis are a pair of gaudily coloured stone lions, which have looked down for a matter of three hundred years on the Pilgrim Fathers, some of whom had gathered and settled here previous to going to the New World, on Oliver Goldsmith, on Boswell, on Evelyn, and on many other Englishmen who attended the famous university here.

One learns that these lions were once properly coloured beasts, — at least of the conventional tone of stone sculptured animals, and that they were only recently painted a gaudy vermilion, which apparently is not a very durable colour, as in these days they seem to shed and don their coats with surprising frequency.

The chief ecclesiastical monuments of Leyden are the church of St. Peter, of the thirteenth to sixteenth century, a vast Latin cross of not very good Gothic; and St. Pancras, of the thirteenth century, built, curiously enough, on the ground-plan of a St. Andrew's cross.

St. Peter's was built in 1221, but in 1512 its great tower fell and was replaced by the present one, which rises high above the rest of the fabric.

In truth, there is not much of interest to be derived from a contemplation of the church except the memory of the great names of those interred therein, which form a veritable category of those who became famous in matters ecclesiastic, artistic, and scientific, in Holland's roll of fame.

Near St. Peter's is a thirteenth-century edifice now used as a prison. In olden times it served as the residence of the Counts of Holland, the name "Gravenstein" on the ancient structure signifying "the house of the count."

The church of St. Pancras is an ogival edifice built in 1280. It has no remarkably artistic attributes, and its chief interest consists in the fact that it contains the tomb of Van der Werf, the courageous burgomaster, who, in 1574, so heroically defended the city. He was born at Leyden in 1529 and died in 1604.

Leyden may be called the learned city of Holland. In recognition of having withstood a siege by the Spaniards of 131 days, the city was given the choice between exemption from taxation or the foundation of a university, and chose the latter.

The city is the birthplace of many men famous in Dutch art, among them Lucas de Leyde, Rembrandt, Gerard Dow, G. Metsu, J. van Goyen.

Here also was born the celebrated anabaptist known as John of Leyden.

THE END.

APPENDIX

CHRONOLOGICAL TABLES AND DIAGRAMS

AIX-LA-CHAPELLE

**ROUND CHURCH IN THE IXTH CENTURY, AIX-LA-CHAPELLE
(DIAGRAM)**

Charlemagne died at Aix-la-Chapelle, 814
Charlemagne's original chapel founded, VIIIth century
Damaged by fire, 1146, 1234, 1236, 1656
Choir begun, 1353
Choir completed, XIVth century
Minorite church, XIVth to XVth century

ANDERNACH

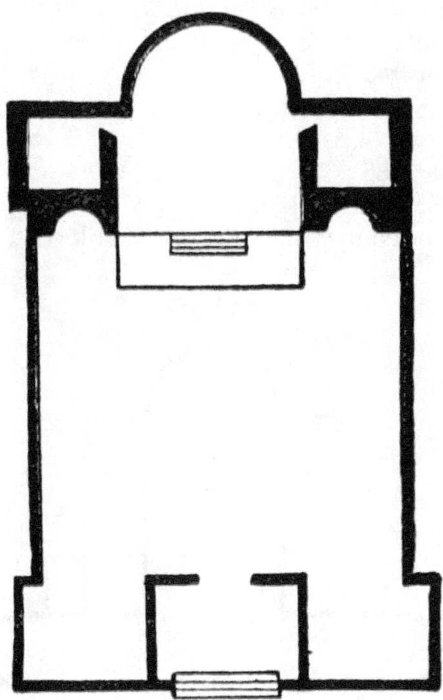

ST. GENEVIEVE, ANDERNACH (DIAGRAM)

Foundation of primitive church, Xth century
St. Genevieve, XIIIth century
Coloured *bas-relief* of portal, XVIth century
Lahnstein tomb, 1541

ARNHEIM

City gave adherence to "Union of Utrecht," 1579
Taken by the French, 1672
Taken by the Prussians, 1813
Groote Kerk founded, 1452
Main portions of Groote Kerk, XIVth and XVth centuries
St. Walburge, XIVth century
Monument of Duke of Guelderland, XVIth century
Maison du Diable (restored 1830), XVIth century

BACHARACH AND BINGEN

Protestant temple, Bacharach, XIIth century
Château of Archbishops of Mayence at Asmanhausen, XIIIth century
"Mouse Tower," XIIIth century

BASEL

Councils of the Church held here, 1061 and 1431
Cathedral founded by Henry II., 1010
Cathedral dedicated, 1019
Bridge crossing the Rhine, 1220
Council-chamber, 1431-44
Baptismal font, 1465
North tower (66 metres), 1500
University founded by bull of Pius II., XVIth century

BONN

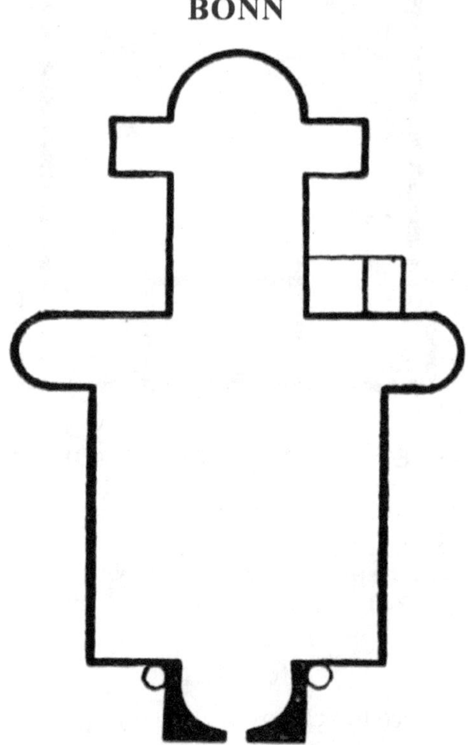

BONN CATHEDRAL (DIAGRAM)

Primitive church founded by the mother of Constantine, 319
Present cathedral choir and crypt, 1157
Main fabric, XIIth and XIIIth centuries
The Electors of Cologne came to reside at Bonn, 1268

BOPPART

Hauptkirche built, 1200 (?)
Carmeliterkirche built, XVIth century
Boppart made a *ville impériale*, XIVth century

CLÈVES

Sacked by the Normans, IXth century

COBLENZ

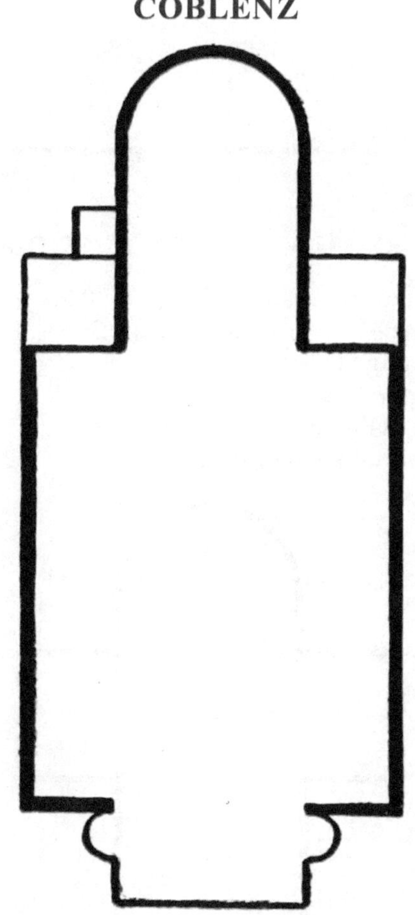

ST. CASTOR, COBLENZ (DIAGRAM)

St. Castor founded by Louis the Pious, 836
Lower ranges of towers, XIth century
Reconciliation of Henry IV. with his sons, 1105
St. Bernard preached Crusades here, XIIth century
Bridge crossing the Moselle, 1344

COLMAR

St. Martin's foundations, XIIIth century
St. Martin's choir, 1315
Virgin of the Roses, XVth century
Dominican Convent of Unterlinden, 1232

COLOGNE

ANCIENT CATHEDRAL, COLOGNE (DIAGRAM)

Romanesque cathedral destroyed by fire, 1248
Foundation-stone of new cathedral laid, 1248
Charter mentioning St. Trond, 1257
Choir consecrated, 1322
Work stagnated, XVth and XVIth centuries
Work again undertaken, XVIIth century

PRESENT CATHEDRAL, COLOGNE (DIAGRAM)

Renaissance details added to choir, XVIIIth century
Napoleon transferred archbishopric to Aix, XIXth century
See reëstablished at Cologne, 1821
Restoration begun and choir reopened, 1842
Reliques of the "Three Kings" first brought from Milan, 1164
Tapestries in choir, XVth century

Glass in Chapel of the Three Kings, XVth century
Organ-case, 1572
Candelabra of choir, 1770
Nave consecrated, 1848
Wall between nave and choir broken out, 1863
Spires of towers added, 1870
Spires completed, 1880
Petrarch visited Cologne, 1331
Marie de Medici died at Cologne, 1642

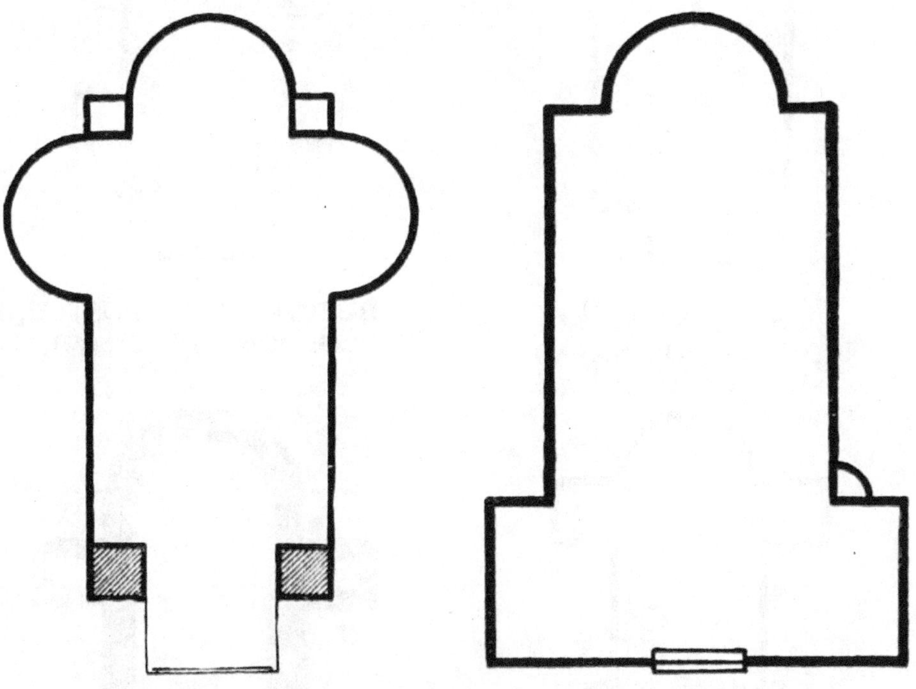

ST. MARIA IN CAPITOLIA, COLOGNE (DIAGRAM)

ST. CUNIBERT'S, COLOGNE (DIAGRAM)

St. Maria in Capitolia (nave), XIth century
St. Maria in Capitolia (apses), XIIth century
St. Pantaleon, 980
Apostles' Church, XIth century
St. Géréon's (primitive church), Vth century
Jews driven from Cologne, 1425
Protestants driven from Cologne, 1618
Abbey of Altenburg (glass), 1270-1300
Abbey of Altenburg (choir), 1255

ST. MARTIN'S,
COLOGNE (DIAGRAM)

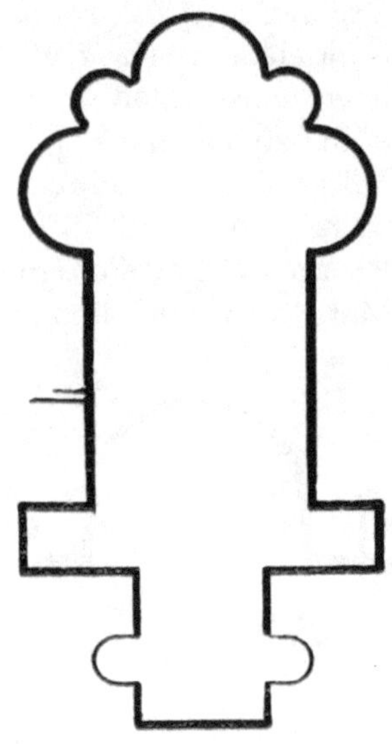

CHURCH OF THE APOSTLES,
COLOGNE (DIAGRAM)

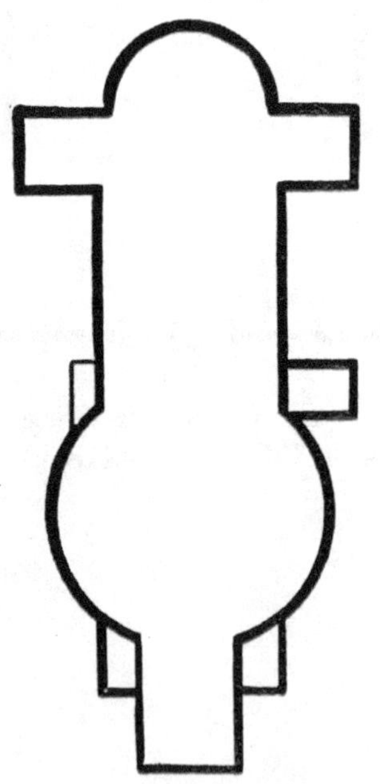

ST. GÉRÊON'S,
COLOGNE (DIAGRAM)

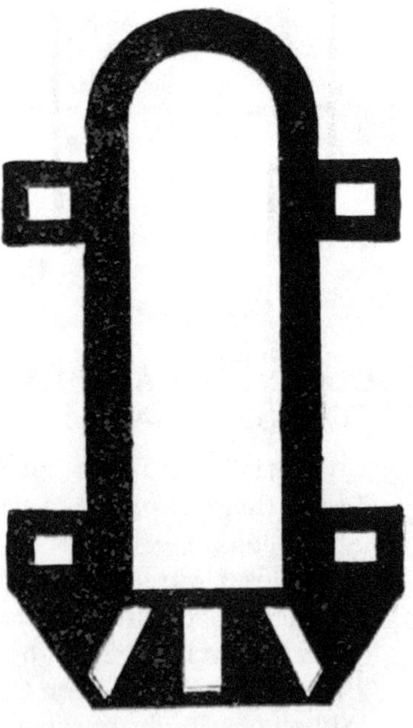

CRYPT, ST. GÉRÊON'S,
COLOGNE (DIAGRAM)

CONSTANCE

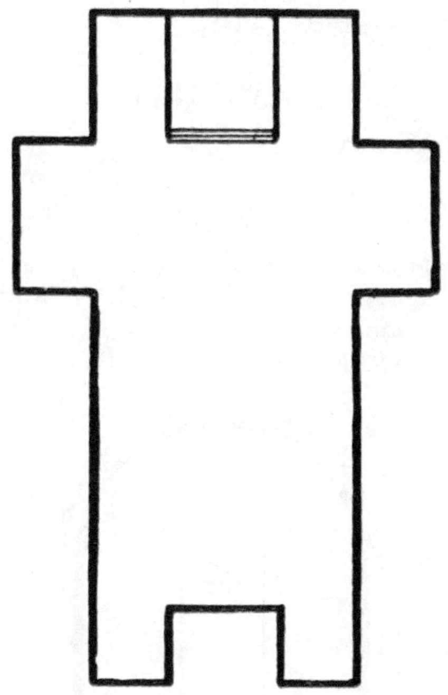

CONSTANCE CATHEDRAL (DIAGRAM)

City founded by Emperor Constance, 297
Ville impériale, Xth century
Peace between Barbarossa and Lombardy, 1183
Cathedral founded, XIth century
Bishop Salomon occupied the see, 891-919
St. Stephen's enlarged by Bishop Salomon, 900
Further embellished by Bishop Conrad of Altdorf, 935
Renovated by Bishop Theodoric, 1047-51
Council-chamber built, 1388
Roof of nave and aisles (in wood), 1600
Council concerning the three popes, 1414-18
Council condemning John Huss, 1414
John Huss burned alive, 1415
Reconstructed by Bishop Otto III., 1428
Consecrated to the Lutherites, 1522-48
Organ and case (restored 1819 and 1839), 1583
Catholicism reëstablished at Constance, 1550

DORTMUND

St. Mary's, XIIth century

St. Reinhold's nave and transepts, XIIIth century
St. Reinhold's choir, XVth century
Pfarrkirche, XIVth century

EMMERICH

St. Martin's Xth century

ESSEN

Romanesque details of cathedral, 874
Crypt, transept, and choir foundation, XIth century
Seven-branched candlestick, 1003
Gothic additions, XIVth century

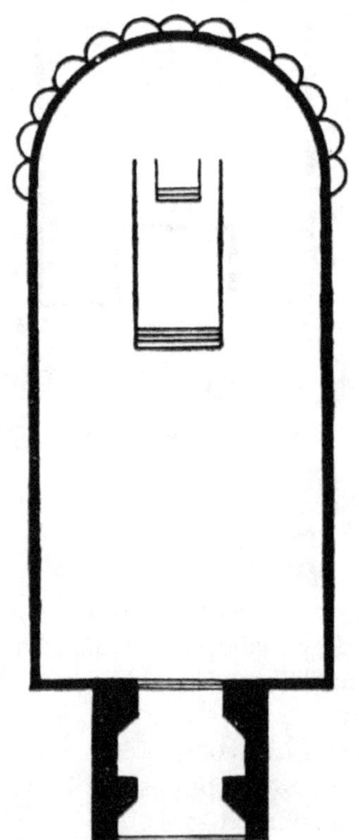

FREIBURG CATHEDRAL (DIAGRAM)

FRANKFORT

First historical mention, 794
Juden Gasse, 1662
Cathedral completed, XIVth century
Tomb of Emperor Gunther of Schwarzburg, 1349

Tomb of Knight of Sachsenhausen, 1371
Late Gothic western tower (163 feet), 1415-1509
Tomb of Consul Hirde, 1518
St. Leonard's, XIIIth century
St. Catherine's XVIIth century
St. Paul's, 1833

FREIBURG

City founded by Berthold III., 1118
Cathedral founded by the same, 1122
Nave and restored choir, XIIIth century
Cathedral finally completed, 1513
Benedictine Convent of Taennenbach, XIIth century
Cloister of parish church, XIVth century

GODESBERG

Given to Archbishop of Cologne, 1210
Chapel of St. Michal, XIIIth century
Château of archbishops pillaged, 1593

HEIDELBERG

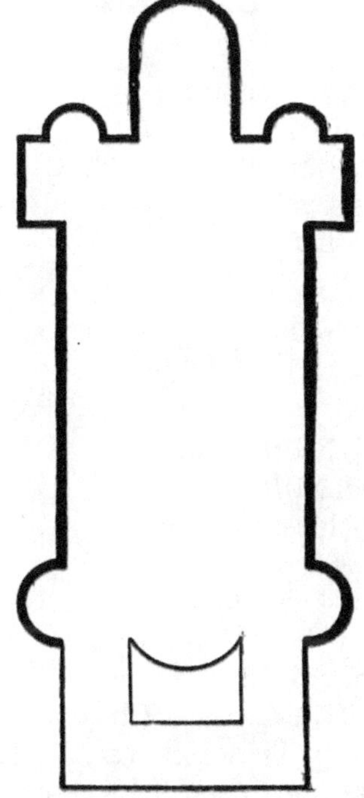

ABBEY OF LAACH (DIAGRAM)

Conrad of Hohenstaufen, first Count Palatinate, 1148
Heidelberg made capital of the Palatinate, 1228
St. Esprit's, XIVth to XVth century
House of the Chevalier zum Ritter, 1492
University of Heidelberg founded, 1386
Luther at the University, 1515
Heidelberg invaded by Tilly, 1622
Library of University given to Pope Leo XIth, 1622
St. Peter's sacked by Mélac, 1693
Library of the Palatine sent from Rome to Paris, 1795
Library returned to Heidelberg, 1815
Castle built by the Elector, Robert I., XIVth century
Additions by Otto Henry, 1556-59
Later additions by Frederick IV., XVIth century
Castle ravaged by Spaniards, 1622
Again rebuilt and dismembered by lightning, 1764
Great tuns, 1535, 1728, 1751

LAACH

Abbey founded by Henry II., 1093
Pillaged by revolutionists, XVIIIth century

LEYDEN

St. Pancras, 1280
St. Peter's, XIIIth to XVIth century
St. Peter's tower fell, 1512
Old Palace of Counts of Holland (1280), XIIIth century
Tomb of Van der Werf in St. Pancras, XVIth century
City besieged by Spaniards, 1574
Stadt Huis, 1597

LIÈGE

St. Jean, Xth century
St. Jean, choir added, XIIIth century
St. Jean, tower added, XIIIth century
St. Jean, cloister, XIVth century
St. Martin founded, 962
Bishopric founded by Héraclius, 968
Ste. Croix founded by Bishop Notger, 979
Ste. Croix, choir added, 1175
Ste. Croix, Stations of the Cross, XVth century
St. Jacques's founded by Bishop Baudry II., 1014
St. Jacques's Romanesque tower, XIIth century
St. Jacques's rebuilt, 1513-38
St. Jacques's organ buffet, 1673

St. Barthélemy's font, 1112
Fête Dieu ordained by Urbain IV., 1246
St. Lambert's destroyed, 1801

LIMBURG

Primitive church, 909
Cathedral of St. George, XIIth century
Baptismal fonts, XIIth century
Baldaquin of Pyx, XVth century
Tomb of Daniel of Mutersbach, 1475

MANNHEIM

City founded, 765
Elector Frederick built his château, XVIIth century
City walls built, 1606

MAYENCE

Bishops of the Frankish kingdom convoked by Dagobert, 636
Bishop Sigibert built the city walls, 718
Council met here on order of Charlemagne, 813
Archbishop Willigis built the cathedral and St. Stephen's, 975-1011
Cathedral completed under Archbishop Bardon, 1037
Pope Leo IX. held a council here, 1049
Cathedral burned, 1087
Philip of Suabia crowned here, 1198
Transept and western choir rebuilt, XIIth century
Chapter-house, XIIth century
Cathedral newly consecrated, 1239
Cloisters, XIIIth century
Chapels, XIIIth and XIVth centuries
Western end of roof took fire, 1793
Napoleon ordered it restored, 1803
Remains of Frastrada (d. 794) removed thither, 1552
Fountain in Speise-Markt, XVIth century

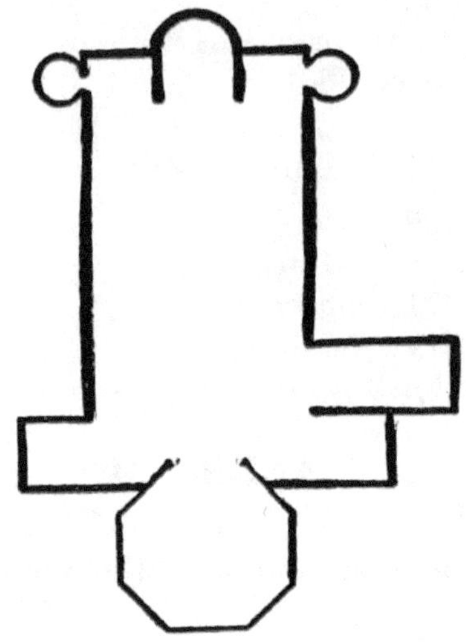

MAYENCE CATHEDRAL (DIAGRAM)

GOTHARD CHAPEL, MAYENCE (DIAGRAM)

METZ

City attacked by the Huns, Vth century
Original foundation of Église St. Pierre, VIIth century
Reconstructed, Xth and XVth centuries
St. Stephen's (cathedral), XIIIth century
Glass of clerestory of St. Stephen's, XVIth century
St. Martin's, XIIIth century
St. Vincent's, XIIIth century
Montmorenci captured the city, 1552

Abbey of St. Arnulphe destroyed, XVIth century
Citadel built, 1556-62

MÜNCHEN-GLADBACH

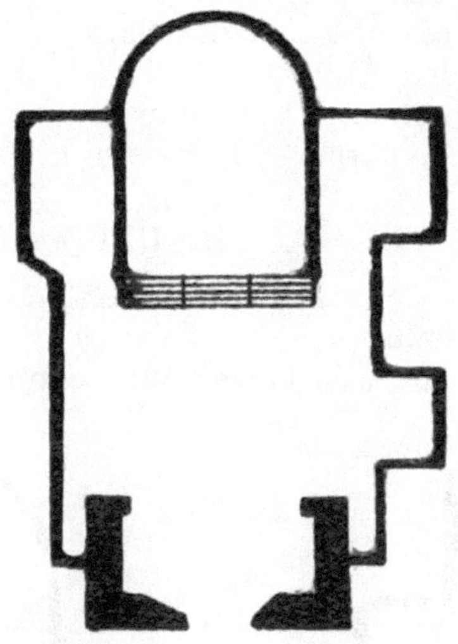

ABBEY CHURCH, MÜNCHEN-GLADBACH (DIAGRAM)

Abbey church, XIIIth century
Stadt Kirche, XIVth century

NEUSS

ST. QUIRINUS, NEUSS (DIAGRAM)

City ravaged by Attila, 451
Chapter of Nobles founded, 825
By the Normans, IXth century
Primitive church founded, IXth century
Collegiate church destroyed, 1199
Under patronage of Archbishop of Cologne, 1206
St. Quirinus founded, 1209
Choir-stalls, St. Quirinus, XIVth century
Cupola frescoes, St. Quirinus, XIXth century

SCHAFFHAUSEN

Abbey founded by Count Nellenburg, 1052
Cathedral, XIIth century
Convent of St. Hilaire at Sackingen, VIth century

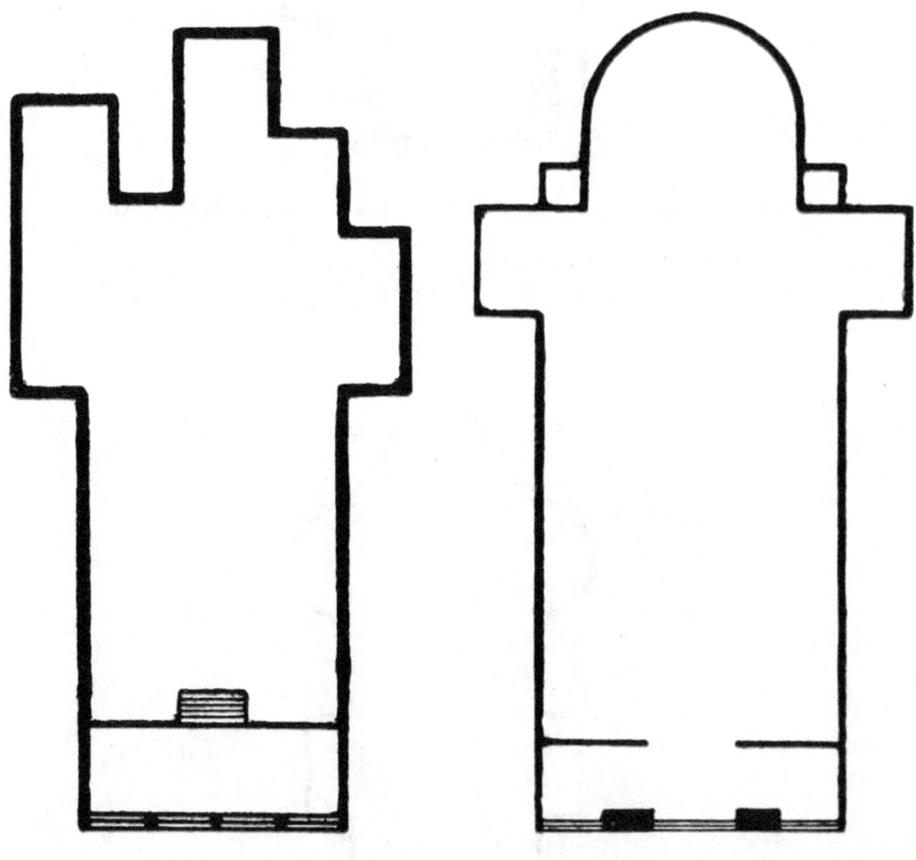

SCHAFFHAUSEN CATHEDRAL
(DIAGRAM)

SPEYER CATHEDRAL
(DIAGRAM)

SPEYER

Foundation of cathedral laid, 1030
Practically completed, 1060
Destroyed by fire, 1159
Rebuilt, 1170
Other fires, 1189-1450
Cloister built, 1437
Burned in the religious wars, XVIth century
Restored, XVIIIth century
Nave restored by Bishop August, 1772
Later restorations, 1823

STOLZENFELS

Castle founded by Arnold of Trèves, XIIIth century
Nearly destroyed by the French, 1688
Given to the Prince Royal of Prussia, 1825

STRASBURG

Primitive church founded by Clovis, 504
Destroyed by fire, 873
Pillaged and fired anew by Duke Hermann, 1002
Present cathedral begun, 1277
Great portal begun by Ervin von Steinbach, 1277
Ervin von Steinbach died, 1318
First Strasburg clock, 1352
Second Strasburg clock, 1571-74
Second Strasburg clock restored, 1669 and 1732
Second Strasburg clock ceased its functions, 1790
Present Strasburg clock inaugurated, 1842
Choir, St. Bartholomew's, 1308-45
"Danse des Morts" (St. Bartholomew's), XVth century
Maison de l'Oeuvre Notre Dame, 1581
Episcopal palace built by Cardinal de Rohan, 1741
Height of spire of cathedrals: Strasburg,
440 feet; Cologne, 482 feet;
Rouen, 458 feet; Paris, 200 feet

TRÈVES

Primitive church founded, 327
See became an archbishopric, XIIth century
Archbishops removed to Coblenz, XIVth century
Holy robe of Trèves brought from Holy Land, IVth century
Tomb of Cardinal Ivo, XIIth century
Notre Dame built, 1227-43

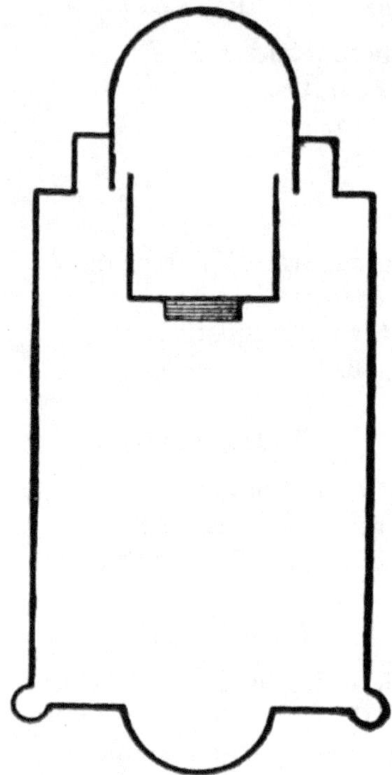

TRÈVES CATHEDRAL (DIAGRAM)

UTRECHT

Primitive church founded by Dagobert, 630
City devastated, VIIth century
City rebuilt by Clothaire IV., 718
Enlarged by Bishop Baldric of Clèves, 934
Adrien Florizoon of Utrecht became Pope Adrien VI., 1522
See made an archbishopric, 1559
Religious reform advocated by Prince of Orange, 1577
States General sat at Utrecht, 1579
Cathedral of St. Martin rebuilt from primitive church, 1024
Cathedral of St. Martin again rebuilt, 1257
Tower, 1331-82
Nave damaged, 1674

WORMS

Concordat between Pope Calixtus II. and Henry V., 1122
Diet of Worms declared Luther a heretic, 1321
Cathedral begun by Bishop Bouchard, 996
Later additions and rebuilding since, 1185

City besieged but cathedral unharmed, 1689
St. Martin, XIIth century
Notre Dame, XIIIth to XIVth century
Synagogue, XIth century
Jewish colony at Worms, 550 B. c.
Abbey of Lorsch founded, 767-774
Primitive church founded at Lorsch, 285
Lorsch incorporated with Archbishopric of Mayence, 1232
Abbey rebuilt, 1100

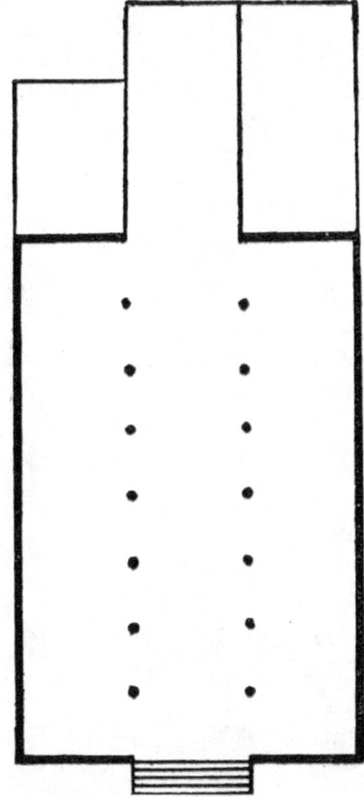

ST. MARTIN, WORMS (DIAGRAM)

XANTEN

Captured by the French, 1672
Collegiate church of St. Victor, XIIth century
Chancel screen, 1501
Monument to Cornelius de Pauw, XVIIIth century

INDEX

A

B

C

Lector House believes that a society develops through a two-fold approach of continuous learning and adaptation, which is derived from the study of classic literary works spread across the historic timeline of literature records. Therefore, we aim at reviving, repairing and redeveloping all those inaccessible or damaged but historically as well as culturally important literature across subjects so that the future generations may have an opportunity to study and learn from past works to embark upon a journey of creating a better future.

This book is a result of an effort made by Lector House towards making a contribution to the preservation and repair of original ancient works which might hold historical significance to the approach of continuous learning across subjects.

HAPPY READING & LEARNING!

LECTOR HOUSE LLP
E-MAIL: lectorpublishing@gmail.com